Self-Publishing

A
Step-by-Step
Guide

MARK McCABE

Serotine Press Australia www.serotinepress.com.au

ISBN: 978-0-6486768-0-5

First Edition

First published September 2019

Author website:
https://markmccabeauthor.com

Serotine Editing and Manuscript Services:
https://serotine-editing.com

ABOUT THE AUTHOR

Mark McCabe is the author of two fantasy novels — *As Fire is to Gold*, and *When All the Leaves Have Fallen*, Books 1 and 2 of the Chronicles of the Ilaroi. A combined volume, *As Fire is to Gold: The Complete Chronicles of the Ilaroi*, has also been released. *Self-Publishing: A Step-by-Step Guide* is Mark's first non-fiction publication.

Mark was born in Brisbane, Australia. He lived for a number of years in Sydney and then moved to Canberra, the Australian capital city, where he completed a career in the Australian Government and Australian Capital Territory's public service agencies. Upon retiring, Mark and his family moved to New Zealand and took up residence near Dunedin.

Mark holds a Bachelor of Arts majoring in Classics, Latin and English from the Australian National University. He now runs an editing business, Serotine Editing and Manuscript Services, providing editing, manuscript assessment, formatting, layout, cover design, and other services, with an emphasis on supporting indie authors.

Mark's favoured genres are fantasy (predominantly epic and high fantasy) and science fiction. He cites Robert Jordan, David Gemmell, Jack Vance, and Ursula Le Guin as key inspirations and influences.

In his spare time, Mark is an amateur photographer and a keen student of the classics, with a focus on the Roman Empire.

Author Website: https://markmccabeauthor.com

Serotine Editing and Publishing Services: https://serotine-editing.com

CONTENTS

FOREWORD

This book came about after I self-published a number of my own manuscripts. When I looked back on the experience, I thought about what a slow process it had been at first, how many things I wish I had known right from the start and all that I had subsequently learnt. I realised how much quicker the process had become as my knowledge-bank had grown. Clearly, this was knowledge and experience other authors could benefit from.

I have published five books now, with the various paperback, hardback, large print and eBook editions I have produced resulting in eleven separate publications. That's eleven times I have been through the publishing process. As you might guess, it happens very quickly for me now. And I know just which steps to put in train long before I get to the end of my manuscript so that the whole process comes together with a minimum of delay.

Although the process is a very straightforward one once you know what you are doing, however, there are plenty of potential hurdles — steps which should be completed in a particular order or which contain hidden twists to trap the uninformed.

The problem is that by the time you find out about a potential twist, you've already wasted some of your precious time and effort. In the worst-case scenario, you may have done something you cannot now undo. Fortunately, these are all pitfalls which can be easily avoided if you are forewarned.

Hence this guide. My goal is to make this book as complete as I possibly can — without it becoming longer than *War and Peace*, or George R. R. Martin's *A Song of Ice and Fire*.

It is for that reason that the final chapters touch on matters which occur post-publication. Whole books have been written about many of the subjects I include there, so I won't try to compete with those. My goal is simply to alert you to some of the issues you will encounter after your book is published. That knowledge may influence some of the decisions you make as you go through the publishing process.

Many of you will not need to follow all of the steps I have outlined in this book, while others will diligently follow every single one. The beauty of self-publishing is that the decision is yours. What you decide to do will depend very much on the nature of your publication, your own goals, and your appetite for investing time and, on some occasions, perhaps a little money too.

Without a doubt, a person can self-publish a manuscript within a matter of weeks, and at no, or very close to no, cost at all — and still produce a quality end-product. The quality is the crucial issue, however. Achieving that requires commitment and care. But isn't that what the manuscript you have lovingly laboured over deserves?

Achieving a quality outcome also requires a bit of knowledge and some skill. The knowledge bit is easily overcome. My intention is for this guide to arm you with that.

The question of skill is where the issue of cost can come in to play, if you want it to. The primary costs you are likely to incur will come from only a handful of matters — if you decide to get a quality Manuscript Assessment from a professional, if you decide to pay an appropriately experienced person to copy-edit your manuscript, and if you decide to pay someone to design a cover for your finished publication.

You can do all three of these things yourself, especially if you have access to friends or colleagues who can help. Let's call that the DIY Approach. A key question if you go down that path will be whether you and those friends and colleagues have the skills to do the required work. Unless they are experienced editors or designers, there is likely to be some diminution in the quality of what your friends can do for you compared to what an external service provider could do.

You can, on the other hand, choose to pay a service provider (or providers) to do some or all of those tasks. Let's call this the Assisted Approach. Whether you do this will depend on your appetite and capacity for spending some dollars to lift the quality of your final publication. Once again, as a self-publisher, you have control over these decisions. This guide will help you make those decisions from a position of knowledge, and with an understanding of the likely consequences.

This guide will also provide you with advice on how to navigate your way through the myriad of service providers out there catering for just these needs. Some are cheap. Some are very expensive. Some are, to put it bluntly, charlatans. Fortunately, many others provide excellent results for a reasonable cost. The trick is to shop around for the most cost-effective providers, seeking out reviews of their work before you engage them and not just jumping in and going with someone who sounds great but ends up letting you down.

Finally, don't be daunted. Self-publishing is not beyond you. The important thing is to take a bit of care and not to rush it — there is no need to. Don't lose sight of the goal of producing a quality product.

I can honestly say that I think you will find the self-publishing process an extremely rewarding one. No doubt, you will face a few frustrations along the way, especially if this is your first time. The rewards and the satisfaction when the first copy of your completed publication arrives, however, will quickly dispel any of those.

Mark McCabe

———————

1. WHY SELF-PUBLISH?

You've finished your manuscript, or you're getting very close to the end, and your mind is starting to turn to getting your work published. The hard work is almost over. Well ... not quite.

I'd like to start this book on a positive note by confirming that all of the work is, in fact, behind you, but I can't. You still have a fair bit to do. How much will depend on the path you intend to follow. Will you try to find a 'traditional publisher' to take your manuscript through to publication, or will you go down the self-publishing path? There is even a third path, but that is one to be avoided at all costs — more about that below.

Be clear on what your goals are and who your likely audience is

Before you even think about which of those paths to follow, you need to consider an even more fundamental question, one that will help you decide which is the best path for you to follow with your manuscript.

It's a simple question — why did you write the manuscript you have written?

Was it because your aspiration is to be a best-selling, or at least a moderately successful, author (really aspire, that is, not just dream of such an outcome as almost every writer does at some point)? Was it simply to scratch an itch? Was it because you have some important knowledge you would like to share with a specific group of potential readers? Was it because you want to share a memoir or all that detail from your family history research with your broader circle of friends and family, or was there some other reason? Do you expect that there will be more to follow? Is this a one-off, or are you already thinking about (perhaps even working on) your next manuscript? What are your realistic hopes and expectations?

Having a good sense of the answers to these questions will help you establish who your potential audience is. This is as important a consideration as the question of why you wrote your manuscript in the first place. If your audience for your memoir or family history, for example, is your own circle of friends and relatives, you may not want to wait the one, two or even three years to find a traditional publisher and work right through their publishing process. Knowing your audience will also help you answer a number of other questions you will encounter along the way. What sort of cover will appeal to that audience, for example, what format and layout, and so on?

Knowing the answers to these questions will also help you decide which of the broad paths which lie before you you should follow. Let's examine the three paths in a bit more detail.

Traditional Publishing

I'll start with traditional publishing, that is, being published by a publishing company. Note that this does not include 'vanity press' or 'subsidy publishing' businesses, which masquerade as traditional publishing houses. That is the third path. More about that below.

Publishing with a major publishing house involves, as a first step, finding the ones that are currently accepting submissions for manuscripts in the genre you have chosen to write in. Once you have identified those publishers (this may not be a very big list), you will then need to submit a query letter or a proposal, along with your manuscript. When they receive your package, your manuscript will go into one of two piles (if you email it to them consider these 'virtual' piles). The priority pile will be for manuscripts from authors who have been published previously, though not necessarily by them. The second pile, which is likely to be a big one, will be for manuscripts from unpublished authors.

As you can imagine, given the likely size of the second pile, the editor who must read those manuscripts and decide whether to offer the author a deal will probably follow a fairly ruthless decision-making process. Many manuscripts will be put aside for a rejection letter after only a few pages or, at best, no more than a chapter. Editors do not have the time to read every manuscript they receive in full and will quickly discard ones they don't think the publisher can make a profit from.

Assuming you are one of the **less than one percent** who makes it through that sifting process, you may then be offered a publishing deal. Book deals typically involve the publisher purchasing all of the rights to your book from you. In return for this, you will receive royalties from any sales. In some cases, you may even receive an advance. An advance, however, is just that — an advance payment against future royalties. If you do receive an advance, you will not receive any further payments until royalties from sales exceed the amount already paid to you.

Perhaps more importantly, the publisher will take on the responsibilities and costs associated with designing, printing, distributing and marketing the book. You will be consulted on most of this, but the ultimate decision will rest with the publisher. Remember, they will have purchased the rights to your book.

The above process is usually a very slow one. Count on anywhere between 12 to 24 or more months before you either get a successful response to one of your query letters/proposals/submissions, or before you decide to give up! Dealing with rejection letters (all authors get them — J. K. Rowling received dozens before finally finding a publisher for her Harry Potter novels) can be very depressing. Many of them will give no reason for the rejection. Some may even be rude. A very few might offer some helpful advice.

Then you need to count on another 12 to 24 months to get through the publication process. Yes — it really can take that long! It is a rarity for the process to take less than 12 months.

If you can make it through all of that, as a traditionally published author, you will not have had to pay anything for your book to be published. The flipside is that the publisher will now own the rights to your book. They will pay you a royalty for every book sold. Average royalty rates are between 8% to 15%, though I've yet to meet anyone who got anything near 15%.

Pros of Traditional Publishing:

- Gives you a lot of 'street cred' in the writer community, though the alternative, self-publishing, is fast becoming recognised as a completely acceptable way to get your book published.
- The publisher will cover any editing, layout and cover design costs (this is one of the biggest advantages of traditional publishing).

Cons of Traditional Publishing:

- You hand over all publishing rights to the publisher, who will then pay you royalties when the books sell. Average royalty rates are between 8% and 15%, as compared to somewhere between 35% and 70% with self-publishing — the publisher has to cover those editing, layout and book cover design costs somehow!
- You may (this does not happen with all publishers) get paid an advance. However, this is an advance against future royalties. Once paid, you will receive no more payments until your total royalties exceed the amount of the advance already paid to you.
- Less than 1% of authors get accepted by a publisher.
- Of that less than 1%, industry figures indicate that only a small percentage (best estimates are around 10%) of this number will make a profit.
- If, after many rejections, you are accepted by a publisher (a process which itself may take up to 12 to 24 months or more), it will most likely take a further 12 to 24 months to get the book published and available in the marketplace, with the real possibility of the publisher deciding to pull out of the deal anywhere along the way (this does happen). This means that you can spend months if not years only to end up with a pile of rejection letters and a still unpublished manuscript. Even established authors cannot guarantee that their next manuscript will be accepted by a traditional publisher.
- You will often find the publisher does a lot less in terms of marketing that you think is appropriate. They are running a business, and every decision to spend money is taken from a business perspective, not from the author's perspective.

- You will often find it difficult to easily access information such as up-to-date statistics on sales from the publisher.
- You may find author copies from a traditional publisher too expensive to make them useful for you to acquire and market yourself locally or otherwise.

Self-Publishing

Self-publishing works a bit differently from traditional publishing. While traditional publishers manage and cover the costs of the entire publishing process, from editing to illustrations to cover design and typesetting, as a self-publisher, you will be responsible for doing all of the work yourself. This does not mean that you *have to* draw your own illustrations, edit your own book, or design your own cover. In fact, you need to be very careful before you think about doing those things on your own.

Some self-publishers pay others to do all of those things, shopping around on the internet or elsewhere for the best deals to keep costs within reasonable bounds. There are some very good providers of these services in the marketplace, some expensive but very good ones, some outrageously expensive ones, many that are cheap, and some that are both moderately priced and who produce excellent outcomes. A bit of research and checking in with writers' associations or writers' groups will help you separate the wheat from the chaff and find someone you can work with — and that you can afford.

Other self-publishers will do some of those things themselves and only pay others to work on the aspects they feel are beyond their skillset.

A smaller number still will do all of it themselves, with quite a considerable cost-saving.

It is quite easy to self-publish a book without incurring any costs at all.

The real issue is achieving sales. The quality of what you publish will have a big part to play in whether your book sells. While many aspects of quality will be determined by the amount of care and effort you put into preparing your manuscript for publication, some, such as cover design, require very specific skills.

Once again, you can produce a good cover for no cost at all. There are a number of sites on the internet which will help you achieve this free of charge. Really good covers, however, come at a cost — anywhere from a few hundred dollars up to around $1500. And covers play an absolutely vital role in achieving sales. As a self-publisher, it is your call how far you go down this track. That decision will depend on your goals for your publication and on your appetite and capacity to invest some dollars in achieving a high-quality end-product.

These issues will be discussed in more detail in Step 4. Suffice to say, at this point, getting tasks that are normally done by professionals done by others (or doing it yourself) will often reduce costs but with the risk of lowering the quality of the final publication. Most of us have limited budgets, however. The trick is to work out how far you can reduce costs without impacting too greatly on quality.

Regardless of the above, one of the major benefits of self-publishing is that it can happen fairly quickly — easily within a few months and potentially even much quicker than that. With a good deal of experience under my belt, I can now publish some of my books within a week, or even a few days. I know just which tasks I need to get underway before I finish my manuscript to achieve that.

A second and arguably more important benefit is that you will retain all of the rights to your own work, as well as control over the whole publishing process from beginning to end.

Finally, none of this is hard to do. It requires a bit of knowledge — this book will provide you with that — and it requires a bit of time and effort, but nothing that is not manageable.

As I have noted above, if you end up publishing more manuscripts down the track, it will get even easier still — and you'll be quicker at it.

You may have flicked through this book and thought to yourself — there are a lot more things I need to do to self-publish my manuscript than I had expected.

Don't be put off.

This book aims to cover every single aspect of self-publishing that can arise, but you don't have to do everything listed here if you don't want to. Some of the matters covered in this book are optional — nice to do if you have the time, or, relevant to some kinds of publications, but not to others. You can follow a cut-down version and get your book published within a few days if that is what suits you, especially if you opt to produce an eBook only and either not publish a print version, or produce one at a later time as suits you.

Pros of Self-Publishing:

- You retain total control over your work.
- All royalties go to you.
- You can easily self-publish within a few months of completing your manuscript. If you get good advice, have done it before, or go for a cut-down approach, it can happen in much less time than that.
- You retain total control over marketing decisions.
- Through print-on-demand services such as Amazon KDP, you can easily access author copies at a very low cost. You can then use these to give away to friends, sell yourself, use in local marketing opportunities, and so on.
- You can still get your books into bricks-and-mortar bookstores, but it takes a bit of effort and time.
- You can get editing, layout and cover design done quite cheaply depending on your own abilities and time available. There will often, however, be a trade-off between financial outlay and quality.
- Profits are just as hard to achieve as they are with a traditional publisher, but control of marketing and promotion lies with you.

- If you are looking at writing as a long-term objective, building up a portfolio of self-published works (assuming you focus on good quality end-product) may help you break down the barriers to the big publishing houses. Only a small number of authors achieve this, but nonetheless, there is a growing number of authors who started out self-publishing and have now hit the 'big-time' with a deal with one of the major publishing houses. Here are just a few:

  ➢ Andy Weir — author of *The Martian* which was self-published in 2011. Crown Publishing purchased the rights to the book in 2014. It has now been made into a major film.
  ➢ E.L. James — author of *Fifty Shades of Grey*, self-published the first book before it took off and achieved worldwide recognition.
  ➢ Libbie Hawker — author of the how-to-plot book, *Take Off Your Pants*, self-publishes her various series but lets her imprint publish her standalones. As you might imagine, this means Libbie is quite prolific. She was on her sixth self-published book when a publisher first approached her. She now has 37 books to her name.
  ➢ Michael J Sullivan — author of *The Riyria Chronicles*, self-published several fantasy novels before being picked up by Orbit.

Cons of Self-Publishing:

- Harder to get your book into bricks-and-mortar bookstores (though they only deliver good sales figures if accompanied by good marketing) but, as noted above, you *can* still achieve this as a self-published author
- You have to pay for editing, layout and book cover design but, as noted above, there are many ways to reduce these costs substantially.

Vanity Press or Subsidy Publishing

The third path is to have your work published by a 'vanity press' or 'subsidy publishing' business. There are publishers who will take a manuscript and publish it at the author's expense. This is, in fact, just another form of self-publishing disguised as traditional publishing. Some subsidy-publishers will provide editorial and proofreading services (which the author pays for), but most take no responsibility for any errors in the text supplied. They also do not get involved in the book's distribution.

These 'publishers' should be avoided at all costs. Writers' associations and others routinely provide lists of specific companies to be avoided. There is no definitive list, however. As soon as they begin to acquire a bad name in the writing community, many of them simply re-badge and then reappear under a different name. They are often associated with outright scams and they prey upon the uninformed. It is not uncommon for their charges to run from anywhere from $5,000 to upwards of $20,000. Some will, in addition to those charges, then take a significant percentage of any royalties as well. They usually don't publish the books themselves, either. Most commonly, they will simply put your book through Amazon KDP on your behalf — something you could have done yourself at no cost at all!

An acquaintance of mine recently decided to publish with one of these publishers. Unfortunately, I did not find out about it until the deed was done and they had already spent several thousands of dollars for something that could have been done just as well at literally no cost at all.

Why pay a subsidy-publisher what can amount to thousands of dollars when you can do all of that yourself, with no great effort other than an investment of a bit of time and care? Who, after all, cares more about your finished manuscript than you?

Yes, doing it yourself requires a bit of skill (computer skills, mainly) and knowledge. That is the aim of this book — to provide you with the knowledge and the skills to do all of the things required.

My first book took me some three or four weeks of work to publish, not counting the considerable amount of time I spent trying to find out how to do it before I started. When I subsequently published a combined version of what had up to then been a two-part story (i.e. it was originally published as two books: Books One and Two of The Chronicles of the Ilaroi), it took me two hours. That was because by then I knew what I was doing! The aim of this book is to put you in a situation where you know what you are doing when you undertake to self-publish your work.

Whoever you decide to deal with, do a bit of research on the internet to see if others have had bad experiences with them. Writers' associations, particularly the pre-eminent national bodies in each country, often publish lists of 'publishers' to be wary of. If a publisher wants to charge you for some part of the deal they are offering you, that can be a warning flag. Check them out thoroughly before you agree to anything.

Summary

Traditional publishing has some advantages (though these are being eroded by self-publishing with every passing year) but is extremely difficult to break into. Even if you can secure a traditional publisher for your manuscript, you may find the final sales and profit outcome is no better (in fact they may very well be worse) than if you had self-published. In most cases, it is also an inordinately lengthy process.

A handful of authors out of the hundreds of thousands if not millions out there hit the big time with their first manuscript. Writing is a craft. Even the most gifted of individuals tend to misfire with their first effort. It is something that writers tend to get better at the more they do it.

Self-publishing is a way to take the first few steps with a relatively small investment of your precious dollars, and without a lot of heartache or sitting around waiting for years for it to finally happen.

It's also a way to begin to build a portfolio of work which you can then use as a springboard if you want to try to build a career as a professional writer.

For the one-off producer of a memoir, a self-help book, or some similar work, it's a very easy way to get that product published and quickly available for others to access or purchase.

The key benefits of self-publishing include:

- **Control:** You will retain ownership of your work and will have complete control over every aspect of your publication. Traditional publishing requires you to hand the rights to your work over to a publishing company for the duration of your contract.
- **Royalties:** You can often make more money by self-publishing and promoting your own work. Royalties from traditional publishers range between 8% and 15%. Royalties for self-publishers range from 35% to 70%.

- **Costs:** Self-publishing is not as expensive as you think it might be. It can even be achieved with no up-front cost at all, though judicious use of professional service providers, within the bounds of what you can afford, will help lift the quality of your publication and potentially significantly boost its marketability. With Print-on-Demand services available from a number of service providers, and digital formats that can be produced at almost zero cost and then made available worldwide within a matter of hours, some of the few benefits of going with a traditional publisher are being quickly eroded.

- **Speed:** You can get your book published and available for purchase within a matter of weeks, at most a few months — as compared to most likely years.

---

2. SELF-PUBLISHING OPTIONS

Once you've decided to self-publish, you will need to consider what options are available for you to do that. In part, this will be linked to what kind of book you intend to publish.

The expected size will be one factor. Amazon Kindle Direct Publishing (Amazon KDP), the current clear market leader, offers sixteen different Trim Sizes (essentially, book size, or the size of the front cover) ranging from 5" x 8" (12.7 x 20.32 cm) up to 8.27" x 11.69" (21 x 29.7 cm). If you intend to publish a 'coffee-table' style book, such as a photographic essay on a particular topic or location, Amazon KDP may not be the service provider that will work for you.

For most fiction and non-fiction books, however, Amazon KDP just can't be beaten. In fact, most of their competitors seem to have given up trying to better them and are now focusing on services that complement what Amazon has on offer.

And Amazon KDP really does what they do very well. Their service is very slick, it's easy to deal with, it's relatively inexpensive, and it offers good returns for authors as well as regular reports which are updated in real-time.

There is no upfront cost for publishing with Amazon.

There is no establishment fee; they simply take a percentage of the royalties from any sales that occur through their distribution network. They offer the author somewhere between 35% and 70% of the royalties, depending upon the particular deal you opt for.

It is, however, up to the author to format, check, edit and otherwise prepare their manuscript (or to get someone to do that for them). It is also up to the author to provide the cover artwork, although, once again, you may decide to engage someone to prepare that for you. Amazon does provide a manuscript template for whatever trim size you opt for. In my case, I was able to use their template to configure my manuscript's print layout without the need for special software (I used Microsoft Word) or any third-party assistance.

With a print publication, or paperback (Amazon KDP does not offer a hardback option at this stage), Print-on-Demand means that, once published, a book is only printed when someone buys it from Amazon's online sales pages, or when you as the author request a number of 'author copies', which are then supplied to you at the Print Cost plus postage.

As the final step before completing the initial publishing process, Amazon advises you what it will cost them per copy to print your book (the Print Cost). You then decide what price it will be sold at (the List Price). The royalties apply to the difference between the Print Cost and the List Price. If my book's List Price is $24.99, for example, and the Print Cost is $6.45, then, if I have chosen the 60% royalty option (more about that in Step 9), my royalty for each paperback sold will be 60% of $18.54 — that is, a royalty of $11.12 per copy.

You can decide on a print edition, or an eBook, or both. Although the print and eBook editions require slightly different formats for both the cover and the manuscript, those formats are closely related. The print edition formats are slightly more complex, and so the usual path is for an author to prepare the files for a print edition first, and then modify the files so that they are suitable for the eBook publication as well.

Significantly more eBooks are sold than are paperbacks, so the eBook option is virtually essential these days — but it is your choice. The profits (royalties) on an eBook are lower as the expectation from buyers is that an eBook will be sold at a significantly lower price than a paperback. In the case of eBooks, rather than estimate a Print Cost, Amazon estimates the cost of producing the eBook and distributing it to the buyer. This cost is deducted from your sale price (List Price) , and your royalty is based on a percentage of the resulting figure.

Along with a range of other useful services, Amazon provide you with an online reporting system and a 'control panel' (called the Bookshelf) to manage any changes to your book (which you can make at any time with no additional charge from Amazon) including, amongst other things, the cover artwork, the content or text, the keywords associated with it, and so on. You can view daily updates of your sales and royalty figures and make changes to the publications price at any time you feel is necessary.

There are, of course, other options than going with Amazon KDP. Many of these offer similar services to those offered by Amazon. None, to date, can match the full range of services offered by Amazon KDP, or their prices.

More importantly, none can match Amazon's domination of the online book sales market. Nearly 70% of all book sales go through them. For my money, unless you are planning a book size that sits outside of what Amazon KDP can deliver, they are the undisputed first-choice service provider for a self-publisher.

Does publishing with Amazon KDP limit your options?

Deciding to avail yourself of Amazon KDP's services does not mean you should not also consider using some of the other providers which nicely complement what Amazon offer.

In terms of a print edition, there are good reasons to consider also publishing with IngramSpark. The latter offer far superior options than Amazon for 'bricks and mortar' bookstores which may want to stock your publication (more about this in Chapter 6). You will need a separate ISBN to upload your book through IngramSpark, but this is easily dealt with (more about ISBNs under Step 5 in Chapter 4).

In terms of eBooks, Amazon KDP is a very significant player, and its Kindle service is hugely popular. Once again, there is no need to make them your exclusive choice, however. Although there is a range of other eBook services, the two standouts in my view are Draft2Digital and Smashwords.

Draft2Digital offers a very slick distribution service to all of the eBook retailers that don't partner with Amazon. Like Amazon KDP, their service also has no upfront charges. They cover their costs by taking a percentage of the royalties on any of your sales through them. Apart from distributing to a wide number of retailers that Amazon doesn't partner with, they also offer some very useful marketing tools that are not provided through Amazon. You will need a separate ISBN to upload your eBook to Draft2Digital (more about this in Chapter 6), but this is easily dealt with.

Smashwords, while not as slick as Draft2Digital, offer even further marketing tools. Once more, there are no upfront charges for publishing your eBook through them. Like Amazon KDP and Draft2Digital, they take a percentage of the royalties on any of your sales through them. And, once again, you will need a separate ISBN to upload your eBook to Smashwords.

Audiobooks

Audiobooks are an alternative to printed books and eBooks which are growing in favour at a very rapid rate. Put simply, an audiobook is a voice recording of the text of your book.

Producing an audiobook, however, is more complex than it might seem. Every chapter and all of the separate front matters, such as the copyright page, the dedication page, and so on, must be produced as a separate file and must fulfil some specific audio requirements such as decibel level, tone, and so on.

Just the task of capturing a quality voice recording alone can be an expensive process. The most common method is to engage someone with a good speaking voice to read the text. Findaway Voices, one of the providers in this field, estimates the cost of a voice recording of 50,000 words of text to be between $1,000 and $2,000. Other sources put the cost of recording 80,000 words at, potentially, upwards of $5,000. Clearly, this is a truckload of money for a self-published author to come up with.

There is a window of hope, however. You can undertake to do the recording yourself.

It will involve a small outlay of dollars to acquire decent quality recording equipment (perhaps somewhere between $100 and $300, though you can spend much more if you choose to). Just speaking into your computer's microphone will not meet the audio requirements any of the respected publishers of audiobooks will require. You need a quality microphone that is fit for purpose, along with some specific attachments or add-ons. You will also need a quiet space free from interruptions to undertake what may be a fairly lengthy recording project.

It will also involve a fairly significant time commitment. It is estimated that an 80,000-word manuscript will take 9 to 10 hours to narrate. But that is an estimate for people who do such narration regularly. You can be sure it will take much longer than that if you do it yourself. Nonetheless, it can be done, and many are now choosing to go down this path. The internet is full of good tips and advice about some of the pitfalls to avoid as well as tricks of the trade that will help you achieve a quality result.

You will need some software to record your efforts and to facilitate management, review and fine-tuning of the recordings you make. Fortunately, you can download free software (Audacity) that will do this from the internet. Apple's Garage Band application, which is provided free of charge with most Apple desktop and laptop computers, will also do the job very competently.

You will also need a separate cover for the finished product which has different parameters than the ones you may have used for your print edition or eBook. An audiobook cover is square. Keep this in mind when you are organising a cover for your print edition and/or eBook, as it will be a simple matter to create a square version suitable for an audiobook at the same time.

Once you have recorded all the necessary files and have reviewed and fine-tuned them to meet the parameters required, there are several service providers that can publish and distribute your audiobook for you. As with print and eBooks, these service providers will then pay you a percentage of the royalties on any sales.

Chapter 9 deals with audiobooks in more detail.

The Best Combination

In my view, having researched these matters thoroughly, and taking into account my own experience after having self-published 11 separate publications, is that the best option is to proceed as follows.

Print Publication

- Publish through Amazon KDP. Use this for purchasing any 'author copies' you require as they are the cheapest provider, especially when the combination of print cost and postage is taken into account. Publishing charge: none other than a percentage of your royalties.
- When that is done, also publish through IngramSpark (refer to Chapter 6 for more on how to do this). Publishing charge: a one-off fee of US$49 plus a percentage of your royalties.
- Once you have published your paperback with IngramSpark as well as Amazon KDP, consider whether there is any merit in publishing a hardback edition as well with IngramSpark.

The combination of Amazon KDP and IngramSpark is also recommended by the Alliance of Independent Authors (ALLi) as offering the widest distribution for your books.

eBook Publication

- Publish through Amazon KDP. Sign up for their KDP Select service for three months (during this period you cannot publish your eBook with anyone else). Utilise the unique marketing options available under the KDP Select service during the three months. Publishing charge: none other than a percentage of your royalties.
- At the conclusion of the Amazon KDP Select three-month period, discontinue KDP Select but otherwise leave you eBook on Amazon KDP.
- Then, upload your eBook for publication through Smashwords as well. This will enable you to access the range of useful marketing

features offered by Smashwords. Publishing charge: none other than a percentage of your royalties.

- Then, upload your eBook for publication through Draft2Digital as well. This will enable you to access the range of useful marketing features offered by Draft2Digital. Publishing charge: none other than a percentage of your royalties.

Audiobooks

- At some future stage, you should at least consider the viability of creating an audiobook edition of your publication. At this stage, only consider this if you are prepared to make a small investment in equipment and a fairly large investment in time to produce and QA the necessary files.

3. SOME PRELIMINARY TASKS

Before you begin the self-publishing process, there are a few preliminary tasks you might want to consider.

Writing Tools

Perhaps one of the most fundamental decisions you will make as a writer is your choice of the software program you will use to draft your manuscript. This choice will have ramifications for how easy, or difficult, it is to prepare a file that you may decide to send off to a professional to have edited, and perhaps even formatted. If you choose to do some or all of the editing or formatting yourself, your choice of software will have some impact there as well.

There are, of course, a range of software programs suitable for drafting a lengthy manuscript. Microsoft Word is probably one of the most commonly used options, though a range of author-specific programs has come on to the market over recent years. Of the latter, the two standouts are Scrivener and Vellum.

I drafted my first novel in Microsoft Word, then used that same program to format the final manuscript and to prepare a file that could be uploaded to Amazon KDP for publishing. It did the job quite competently.

Since then, I have discovered Scrivener and Vellum. For many, these are alternatives choices — that is, you use either Scrivener or Vellum instead of, say, Microsoft Word. Increasingly, however, many are opting to use both of these applications — drafting their manuscript in Scrivener and then formatting it in Vellum.

Scrivener is, in my view, by far and away the best program for drafting a lengthy manuscript. While it is very feature-rich, even the basic functions far exceeded the productivity offered by Microsoft Word. Without going into great detail here, Scrivener's primary benefit is that it allows you to hold all of the information, notes, research, templates, internet links, and so on for your project within the one-program, switching from one to the other with a single click or even splitting the screen so that you can see your notes, for example, on a particular character's quirks or projected journey side-by-side with the text for the scene you are working on.

Amongst its many other features is a tool which allows you to 'storyboard' your plot and any sub-plots. Moving paragraphs or whole sections of your work from one part of your manuscript to another is also a far simpler process in Scrivener than, say, in Microsoft Word.

Scrivener is designed in a way that makes it equally appropriate for authors of all kinds — short story writers, non-fiction and fiction novelists, playwrights, screenwriters, lawyers, students, and so on. The company behind the product is so confident you will like their product they offer a 30-day free trial, with the 30 days being actual days of use as compared to consecutive days.

Scrivener can, at first glance, seem daunting, but most people who spend a little time with it seem to get the hang of it fairly quickly. If you are considering switching to Scrivener, I would suggest you try it. Have a look at one of the myriad of YouTube clips providing overviews of its features before you commence, then start with the basic functions and build your knowledge and use of the more advanced features as and when you require them. I suspect that within a few days of use you, like me, will never go back to what you were using previously.

Its real strength lies in its use as a tool to compose or draft your manuscript. While it has the ability to format the end result, it does not do that as well as, say, Vellum does. On the other hand, while Vellum is an adequate program to use for drafting a manuscript, its real strength lies in the ease with which you can format the end result, be that for a print edition or for an eBook.

And so, my choice, and one which a number of authors seem to have made, is to use Scrivener to draft my manuscript and then, when it is completed, Vellum to format the end result and prepare the necessary files for publishing.

A second program worth mentioning is Grammarly. Grammarly can be used in conjunction with Microsoft Word or with Scrivener. It checks your grammar (including spelling and punctuation) as you go. There is a free version, which is very useful in its own right, or an advanced version which attracts a monthly fee. The advanced version, as you might expect, contains a superior grammar-checking tool to the free version. My advice is, if you do nothing else, get the free version. If you want to go for the advanced version later on, you can then update to that at any time of your choosing.

Getting your choice of the basic drafting tools, such as Scrivener and Grammarly, or whatever combination you decide to go with, right can make life as a writer much easier down the track. As with most skills, choosing the right tools can be the foundation for securing a quality outcome.

Creating and Maintaining a Style Sheet

It's also a good idea to prepare and maintain a Style Sheet as you draft your manuscript. This is where you keep a record of the way you approach a whole range of issues, including:

- Your approach to numbers. Do you, for example, write the word for numbers up to and including nine, and then use actual numbers for everything above nine, or do you spell the word for all numbers?
- When you use an em dash (—), do you put a space on either side or use it with no space?
- Similarly, when you use an ellipsis (…) do you put a space before the first dot and after the last dot, or do you use it without any space between it and the words on either side?
- What is the size of your normal paragraph indent?
- What is the font and font size for a normal paragraph and for headings?
- Do you have a preferred way of capitalising the first letter of the first word of each chapter? Do you use Drop Caps there, for example?

- What country's dictionary do you use for spelling (e.g. US, British, Australian, New Zealand, etc.)?
- How do you deal with a character's thoughts? Do you use italics or some other indicator?
- Do you punctuate dialogue with a single quotation mark (') or a double quotation mark (")?
- What is the correct spelling for certain unusual or uncommon character or place names in your manuscript, including any pronunciation indicators that are required, such as umlauts (ä, ö, ü) or other similar indicators?
- Do some characters have unique nicknames or other shortenings of their name?
- Are there any unique flora or fauna with particular names that must be used consistently?
- Do you have any specific terms that you use for, say, seasons, years, other dates, etc.?
- Are there any other terms or word uses in your manuscript that may be different from what is normally used?

This is unlikely to be a large list. It will, nonetheless, be invaluable, serving at least two purposes. First of all, as the writer, you will find it a useful aid as your manuscript progresses. Depending on the genre you are writing in, it can be hard to remember all of the unique expressions or word uses you decide upon as your story progresses. By adding each one to your Style Sheet, and keeping it available as a quick reference, this problem can be easily overcome, saving you from having to search back through the document to see how you handled the same issue previously.

The second use will be as an aid to the editing of your completed manuscript, be that by someone you have hired, or by yourself. If you have engaged someone to do the work on your behalf, providing them with your style sheet will not only make their job easier, it will ensure that they don't waste time changing words, punctuation or grammar that you purposefully chose to use in a certain way.

Local Writers' Groups

If you haven't already done so, join your local writers' group. Almost every locality has at least one; many will have several. If you can't find one, try an internet search or see if there is a noticeboard at the library or one of your local bookshops — writers' groups often post flyers in such locations. Failing all of that, contact the national writers' association and ask them about any local writers' groups. There is a very high chance they will have all the contact details for such groups on their website.

Local writers' groups, of course, vary in quality and usefulness from location to location. Their members tend to range from 'dabblers' right through to serious, perhaps even published, writers. Nonetheless, they are a potential source of like-minded people attempting to work their way through similar issues to the ones you are confronting.

In all likelihood, some of their members will already have dealt with traditional publishers. Some may have gone down the self-publishing path. Members of these groups are usually only too happy to share those experiences with their colleagues. Just remember to filter what they say. Many of them will only be too eager to tell you what happened to them — but it will be from their perspective.

Writers' groups are also an excellent place to find other writers who may be willing to help critique your work, even if only in small parcels. Critique sub-groups can be an excellent opportunity to get some relatively unbiased feedback on what you have written. Once again, it is not the same as getting feedback from a professional Manuscript Assessor or a Developmental Editor. But it can be a good place to start before you decide to seek more professional advice.

With luck, you will find a group with some members willing to act as 'beta readers' for each other. A beta reader is usually an unpaid test reader of an unreleased work of literature or other writing, who gives feedback to the author from the point of view of an average reader. A beta reader is not a professional and can therefore provide advice and comments in the opinion of an average reader. This feedback is used by the writer to fix remaining issues with plot, pacing, and consistency. The beta reader also serves as a sounding board to see if the book has had the intended emotional impact.

There are also a large number of Facebook groups specifically related to the self-publishing experience, with either local, national or international memberships. These can be excellent sources of advice and opinions. Once again, such advice needs to be taken with a grain of salt. The nature of these groups is such that you will most likely never have met the person giving the advice and you will have no idea whether you would trust them to look after your cat than you would to give you advice about the self-publishing process. As long as you filter the advice judiciously, however, this can be one of your best sources of independent advice on the self-publishing process.

A word of warning, however. The pages of the Facebook groups that are devoted to book cover design abound with posts from members who have clearly paid good money for some professional cover design work and who then, before they finalise their cover, post it on Facebook seeking the views of others.

The people offering those views remain, to all intents and purposes anonymous. They have no idea what discussions have occurred between the author and the cover designer, or what the author's brief to the designer was. More importantly, they are not likely to be experts in cover design. Why pay good money to avail yourself of the services of a professional and then ask the man-in-the-street whether you should accept the resulting product?

Whatever you do, do not rely on feedback from friends and family! They are not only unlikely to be a true representation of the readers you are hoping to target, but are also unlikely to give you objective feedback. In fact, their opinions could very well be totally at odds with your target audience for the genre your work sits within.

National Writers' Associations

National Writers' Associations invariably provide their members with an array of useful information and resources — everything from details of writing competitions, list of local writers' groups, contract advice, lists of reputable service providers and advice on how to navigate your way through the publishing world, just to name a few of the services commonly available.

A particularly useful offering which is quite common to many such associations is either a free or a reduced-cost manuscript assessment of a small portion of your manuscript. This can vary from perhaps ten pages up to a chapter or two.

The majority of these associations offer associate membership for unpublished authors, student membership and full membership for published authors.

They really are one of the best resources you can tap into. Their sole role is to help their members, that is, to help writers. And their advice is objective — unencumbered by links to commercial bodies or considerations.

Set a budget and track all expenditure and revenue

The final preliminary task I recommend is for you to set a budget for your self-publishing project. This may begin as a work-in-progress until you can accumulate enough information to get a clear picture of the likely total cost of your project, but that is fine — you have to start somewhere.

Include in it all of your likely costs, both known and anticipated. As the anticipated cost estimates become clearer, adjust them accordingly. Provide space for the inclusion of revenue once your manuscript has been published, that is, for royalty payments from sales or other income that may be generated.

This will enable you to keep a close eye on your expenditure, monitoring it as it progresses and making informed choices which enable you to keep it within the bounds of what you can afford. It will also be an invaluable record of what you spent on what components of the process should you decide to publish more books down the track.

Keep a copy of all receipts, invoices and estimates.

Tax Deductions

Check with your country's tax agency whether you can claim any of your self-publishing expenditure, as well as any of the broader costs you may incur as a writer, as a tax deduction. If your goal is to earn income from sales of what you have written, you may very well be entitled to claim such expenditure.

The rules on this will vary from country to country.

A logical place to start is with the government body that calculates and collects tax in your country. Don't be surprised if their advice is vague or obscure, however. Tax deductions for authors are unlikely to be a very common issue for such agencies.

Perhaps ask your national writers' association whether they know the answer to this question. Failing that, try some of the Facebook groups of writers from your country.

In my case, I first sought advice from the taxation department in my home country. Their advice was a bit ambiguous. Then I tried one of the primary writers' Facebook groups in my country. Sure enough, I quickly found some writers who had claimed such deductions successfully and who were able to advise me what requirements I would need to meet to substantiate such claims. While I won't take this as definitive advice, it was enough to confirm the wisdom of my decision to keep all of my receipts and other related records.

———————

4. THE STEP-BY-STEP GUIDE

STEP 1 — FINISH YOUR MANUSCRIPT

This book is not a guide on how to write. Though I will touch on some matters that are relevant to the way you have written your manuscript, the assumption is that you've drafted one, or you've almost finished drafting one, and you are either ready to publish, or you are starting to think about publishing your work.

Pictures, Maps, Charts, Diagrams, Etc.

Before you finish your manuscript, you need to decide whether there is any additional material that you want to include. This could include maps, photographs or other images, charts, diagrams, tables, and so on.

You will need to include this material before you can consider the manuscript finished. Importantly, for each item, you need to decide:

- where it will be placed (e.g. on what page, or even where exactly on a particular page; will it, for example, sit alone on a dedicated page)
- what format it will take (this is particularly so for any diagrams or charts)
- whether it will be in colour or black and white (noting that introducing colour to your manuscript will impact on the cost of publishing, which in turn will impact on the price you need to set for the finished work in order to still make a reasonable profit; because of this, black and white is the preferred option wherever possible).

If you are formatting the finished manuscript yourself, you will need to place the item in its appropriate location. If you are engaging someone else to do the formatting, you will need to provide them with all the information they need to either create the item or place it exactly where it is intended to go.

If you are including a map of a country or world, as, for example, may suit a fantasy novel, allow for the time it takes to have the map drawn up. In many cases this will be done by a third party, at a small cost — perhaps $100 or more, depending on the detail required and the skill of the creator. More importantly, allow for the time it will take to have the map drawn up. This could easily be anything from a few weeks to a few months, depending on how busy the mapmaker is, or how complex the map.

You can avoid any delay of this nature by having the map drawn up before you have finished the manuscript. Be wary of having it drawn up too early, however. Should the editing process, or some other late revision of the story, require a change to any place names or the geography of the place or world involved, this could result in more money having to be spent on amending a map that has already been drawn up and paid for.

Once again, avoid colour and wherever possible, opt for a black and white map. They usually look better than colour maps anyway!

It should be noted that tables, in particular, can be problematic if not dealt with correctly. Take special care when reviewing any proof of the proposed final layout (more about this in Step 10) to check all tables, diagrams, and the like very closely. Such items can easily become corrupted during the transformation from the file containing the manuscript to the files that are produced for uploading to the publisher.

Consistency and credibility of approach to the passage of time

Before you finish your story, you should review it to consider consistency and credibility with regard to timelines involved in the story. It is very easy when you are writing a story to initially focus more on what is happening to the characters, and to the all-important plot you are developing or unfolding, than on matters such as consistency and credibility.

Many (probably most) stories involve journeys in some way or other. Many also involve parallel plotlines, or sub-plots, where certain characters are doing one thing at the same time that other characters are doing something else.

Check that these parallel or overlapping timelines have consistency and credibility. To give you an extreme example, if one plotline involves a character flying from London to San Francisco, while the other involves someone else, having dropped the first character off at the airport, returning to their home on the other side of London, the character returning to their home will probably arrive at their destination long before the character flying halfway around the world arrives at theirs. Your story may need to accommodate for this variance in some way.

The easiest way to get around potential problems of this nature is to keep a rough timeline for each separate storyline. This will enable easier identification of where and when those storylines might credibly intersect.

In my fantasy novel, *As Fire is to Gold*, a female character escapes from a villain and makes her way, with a companion, through a wilderness area riding a horse. The villain engages a team of people to find and catch her. This team sets out from a different starting point.

My story followed the journey of the female character and her companion as one storyline. The attempt by the team appointed to catch her is described in a separate, parallel storyline. After several days, the team trying to catch her do find her, and the two storylines intersect. I won't say here what the outcome of that encounter is.

The point is that, in order to maintain credibility, I had to calculate how far each of the two groups could reasonably be expected to travel each day, given their particular circumstances, how many days it would take, therefore, for their paths to intersect., and where that could credibly happen. While this was not a difficult exercise, it was a necessary one to ensure that the story's credibility was maintained. Apps, such as Aeon Timeline, facilitate the tracking of separate character timelines for purposes just like the one I have just outlined.

The internet can also be a useful aid in such matters. You might, for example, have to calculate how far a person can travel each day riding a horse, as in the example above. If you have never ridden a horse, this might seem an impossible task. The internet, however, is an easy source of information of this kind. The only proviso I would add is to check more than one source of such information before trusting its accuracy.

Another trick, if your story is set in the real world and a character (or characters) for some reason has to walk, for example, from London to Portsmouth, is to use Google Maps. Google Maps will tell you that the fastest route, using the A3, will take just under two hours by car. Now click on the walk symbol (or the bike symbol if your characters are going to cycle). Google Maps indicates that it will take just under 24 hours of continuous walking to complete that journey. That probably realistically means at least five to seven days at best, unless your characters are very fit and can walk for more than six hours a day, day after day.

The same issues that apply to distances travelled apply to the weather and matters such as lunar cycles. Have you described a scene in which a full moon illuminates a landscape at some stage during the night and then, two weeks later, a full moon is still shining down upon your characters? Make sure you have allowed for the passage of lunar cycles and other similar matters. It is a simple thing to record in your Style Sheet what lunar cycle you have described, should that occur, and in what scene or scenes at what time intervals. You can then check back to this if you decide to describe the appearance of the moon again in a later scene.

The passing of the seasons is another issue easily overlooked. Unless you are writing *Game of Thrones,* where winter is always coming, if your characters are involved in a scene that is described as occurring at the beginning of spring, by the time six months or so passes by, they are going to be well into autumn. Seemingly small issues such as these, when done right, can add verisimilitude to your story. More importantly, when you get it obviously wrong, an otherwise well-written story can start to feel hollow to your audience. Although you may be writing fiction, the unspoken bargain between author and reader is that the story will be told in a way that allows the reader to 'suspend their disbelief'. Mistakes such as these undermine that bargain.

A simple matter such as the weather can also add to a story's credibility when portrayed in a realistic manner. If your story takes place over a reasonably lengthy period of time, it will generally be unrealistic, for example, for the characters to encounter unrelenting sunny days. In the real world, even in times of drought, there will most likely be some windy days, cooler days, cloudy days, and so on, along with the bright sunny days.

You can get away with a consistent pattern to the weather to some extent. We have all experienced fairly lengthy periods of pleasant weather at times, just as we have experienced lengthy periods of miserable weather. Be careful of overdoing it, however, or of portraying that kind of weather simply because you have been too lazy to describe some variation. It is very easy to get so caught up in the progression of the plot and what is happening to the characters, that you forget about the progress of the seasons and the usual pattern of variations in the weather. This is something you may sometimes only pick up on your second, third or subsequent drafts.

Characters

If you're writing a novel, go back and have a look at your characters. Do individual characters act in a manner that is consistent with the quirks, skills, biases and other attributes you have given them? If they do sometimes act out of character, is there a reason for this and is it credible?

Are the various characters, particularly the more important protagonists, individuals, or do they all act and talk the same? Ideally, some of your characters should be identifiable to your readers just from their dialogue alone.

One of the most common failings I have seen in novels from first-time authors is the tendency of all of their characters to have the same sense of humour and to use almost identical language — and I don't mean English! Real people often tend to use a few words or expressions that are different from those used by others, little idiosyncrasies in their speech that they pick up as a result of their own particular life experiences. This is just one way that you can individualise your characters.

Expectations and Characteristics of the Genre

A further matter to consider before you finalise your manuscript is whether you have paid attention to the characteristics and expectations of your target audience or of stories in your chosen genre. This is not to say that you must stick to rigid rules that apply to specific audiences and genres. It is more a matter of being aware of what the general expectations are, so that if you decide to follow a different path, you do so consciously, having considered the likely response.

Hopefully, you will have been doing this from the outset. Many writers choose to write a story in a particular genre because it is a genre they themselves enjoy and are familiar with. If that is the case, you will probably be very aware of its characteristics, even if only subconsciously.

The type of characteristics I am talking about are not limited to the way stories are usually told. Average word counts for a novel, for example, can vary from genre to genre. While the following word counts will give you a rough guideline for some of the more common genres, these figures are not set in stone, and advice can vary. Do your own research on the internet if you want to explore this matter further.

- *Short Story*: Under 500 words is usually described as 'Flash Fiction'; between 1,000 and 6,000 words is a Short Story, and from 6,000 to 10,000 words is a Long Short Story.
- *Novella*: This is generally a story that is between 10,000 and 40,000 words.
- *Novel*: Usually over 40,000 words.
- *Adult Fiction*: Usually between 80,000 and 100,000 words.
- *Science Fiction*: Usually between 90,000 and 120,000 words
- *Fantasy*: As with Science Fiction, usually between 90,000 and 120,000 words, though many fantasy readers, particularly fans of epic fantasy, will look for stories that are up to 150,000 words, or more. Even better if the book is one of a series that continue the same tale or involve the same characters or world-setting.
- *Romance*: Usually between 50,000 and 100,000 words
- *Historical Fiction*: Similar to Science Fiction and Fantasy, though the average is probably around 100,000 words.

- *Crime/Mysteries/Thrillers/Horror*: Usually between 70,000 and 90,000 words.
- *Young Adult Fiction*: Usually between 50,000 and 80,000 words.
- *Non-Fiction*: These can be anything from 40,000 words upwards, depending on the topic. Do your research for the field you are writing in.

It's also worth looking at how the bulk of novels in the genre you have chosen are presented. What are the norms for chapter length, for the way chapters and headings are presented, and so on? Once again, whatever the norms, they can be, and often are, broken. They are not rigid rules. Nonetheless, once aware of them, you may decide that aligning your own novel to some of them will help to fulfil readers' expectations. This is another of those decisions that you need to consider before you finalise your manuscript.

Save a copy of your manuscript before you start any further editing

I apologise if this is 'telling you how to suck eggs', but it is important. Save a copy of your manuscript file before you begin any further editing. That way you will always have a 'clean' copy to go back to if you want to undo some of the editing changes you make, but for some reason, the program you are using, or some other barrier, is preventing that from happening.

STEP 2 — EDITING

Once you have completed your manuscript, your next task is to decide how you are going to go about getting it edited. This is potentially one of the most expensive tasks you will have to undertake prior to self-publishing, along with getting a good cover design for your completed work.

Of course, if you go down the traditional publishing path, and if you are one of the less than one percent who then secures a traditional publishing deal, your publisher will pay for both the editing and the cover design. A self-publisher, however, has to either complete these tasks themselves or find someone who can do these for them.

Why your manuscript must be edited

All manuscripts need to be edited. The question is how thorough an editing job you choose to get done. Even the best authors submit their work to this process, and many subsequently find that they need to make substantial changes to their original manuscript. This can be a difficult but necessary process — difficult because, by the time you have completed your manuscript, you will most likely have built a fairly close relationship with your work. Standing back and asking someone to critique it is not an easy thing to do.

The very closeness that develops between an author and their work, however, is one of the primary reasons an objective edit of the completed manuscript is so necessary. This is particularly true for issues such as spelling and minor grammatical errors, but often also applies to broader issues such as structure, consistency, balance, and so on. Because you know what you intended to say, it is often hard to objectively assess whether what you have written does, in fact, convey that. Ultimately, of course, the reader will be the final judge of what you have written.

Your manuscript, therefore, simply must be edited. Fortunately, like most tasks in the self-publishing process, you can choose how much, or how little, you want to invest in this process. Many of those on a tight budget will do all of this work themselves. Others will engage a professional editor and get a full edit of the complete manuscript. Still others again will go for a manuscript appraisal of a few chapters and then apply what they learn from that process to the rest of the manuscript. These are just a few of the options open to you. Depending on the path you decide to follow, the cost of the editing process can range from as little as nothing right up to $1,500 to $2,000.

As with all such decisions, however, choices inevitably come with consequences. Once again, it is a trade-off — spend a fair bit of money and get the best outcome possible or spend very little for an outcome that will be of lesser quality but fits within your available resources. Think back to your goals for writing your manuscript when you make this choice. Are you in this for the long haul, with a long-term goal of establishing yourself as an author of merit, or is this a one-off effort you simply want to see brought to completion, or do you have some other goal that lies between those extremes?

If you are in it for the long-haul and want to establish yourself as an author of some credibility, try to find the funds to have your work properly edited. It will not only improve the final published work, but you will also most likely learn a great deal from whatever changes your editor recommends.

Writing is, after all, a craft. Like any craft, you get better at it the more you do it. Even the best writers will tell you they are constantly learning and improving. Just have a look at the Acknowledgements Page in some of the novels you like and see how often good writers pay tribute to the work done by their editor. Few authors, if any, are 'born' perfectly formed. Having your work independently edited is an invaluable part of the learning process.

Is your manuscript ready for editing?

There are some basic questions you should ask yourself before you consider getting your manuscript edited. Editing can be an expensive process, so you don't want to outlay funds if it is not ready to be edited, or if there is more that you could do first to put it into the best shape that you can.

First off, do a word count. Then have a look at some of the suggested normal word counts for manuscripts in the genre you are writing in (as a starting point, have a look at the suggested word counts on pages 32-33 of this book). If you are way over those counts, then it is likely your manuscript is too long. Go back and see if it needs tightening up in places.

There is an old saying in writing circles: if it doesn't progress the plot or any of the character arcs, then get rid of it. That may be a bit harsh, but sometimes you need to be prepared to ditch some of your precious words, as painful a process as that can be. If they aren't really necessary, then there is a good chance they will be slowing down the pace and detracting from the overall quality of your book. Try to be an objective critic of your own work. Have you over-described a place or a scene? Have you allowed some of the dialogue to go on for longer than was necessary?

"For any writer, the ability to look at a sentence and see what's superfluous, what can be altered, revised, expanded, or especially cut, is essential. It's satisfying to see that sentence shrink, snap into place, and ultimately emerge in a more polished form: clear, economical, sharp."

Francine Prose, an American novelist.

The second question is whether this is your first draft. Only a genius can turn out a masterpiece in just one draft. Go back over it and revise it where necessary. This might have to happen several times as you slowly hone and fine-tune what you have written. All good writers do this.

"The function of the first draft is to help you figure out your story. The function of every draft after that is to figure out the most dramatic way to tell that story."

Darcy Pattison.

In his own inimitable style, Ernest Hemingway was somewhat more succinct:

"The first draft of anything is sh_t."

Once you've completed several drafts and you think it is complete, put it aside for a while before you go back and have another look. I don't mean just a few hours. Try to put it aside for a few weeks at least, if not longer — long enough for you to come back to it with fresh eyes and to see if you are still happy with it then, or if it needs a bit more work here and there.

This might seem like a lot of time and effort, but remember, once it is published, it will be out there in the public arena for a very long time. You owe it to yourself, and to your prospective readers, to make it the best that you can.

Finally, show it to someone else. By this stage, you will probably be too close to it to stay objective. You need someone else's opinion. Don't, however, and I can't stress this enough, rely on the opinion of family members or friends. You need someone who will be prepared to tell you if it needs a lot more work, or perhaps just a bit more fine-tuning. Have a look at the section below on critique groups and beta readers. These can be an invaluable aid in getting an objective assessment of what you have written.

Manuscript Assessment or Appraisal

Once you are ready to get your work edited, a manuscript assessment or manuscript appraisal is one of the first steps you can take along the editing path. You don't have to start here, but if this is your first book, it can be an excellent way to begin, particularly if you opt for a partial assessment initially.

A manuscript assessment looks at your work with an eye for the bigger picture. Rather than focusing on spelling and grammar, it considers the structure, content and style of your manuscript. It is sometimes known as a 'structural' or 'substantive' edit. It may include matters such as plot, character, point of view, pace, writing style, narrative, dialogue, presentation, length, use of research, readership, and even marketing or publishing possibilities.

Manuscript assessments differ from copy editing or proofreading. The latter tend to look in detail at the accuracy of things like spelling, grammar and punctuation, while a manuscript assessment will give you professional advice on the work as a whole. A manuscript assessment may tell you that your work needs some editing or proofreading, but it won't provide this service for you. Its purpose is to give you an objective and comprehensive assessment of your work from an experienced professional.

Literary agents or publishers will usually insist that you get a manuscript assessment done before they will consider representing you. Even if you decide to go down the 'indie' route and self-publish, an assessment of this nature can be invaluable. You want to ensure that what goes out under your name is as professional as you can make it.

There are options in respect of such assessments. Some editors will offer a partial manuscript assessment. This might involve them looking at 10 or 20 pages, or just one or two chapters. For a relatively low cost, such an assessment will often uncover some very basic issues which you can then address in the rest of your manuscript.

Partial assessments of this nature are often on offer through national writers' associations at very reasonable prices. They can be an excellent way of identifying and addressing any fundamental issues with your manuscript before you decide whether to spend more money on the editing process. Shop around and see what deals are available in your local area or in your country before dipping your toe in the water.

Critique Groups and Beta Readers

Another option is to join a critique group and work with others to provide objective assessments of each other's work. Your local writers' group may have a critique sub-group. If so, I recommend that you join it and participate. Even the act of critiquing the work of others helps to inform your own work. While this is no substitute for having your manuscript reviewed by an experienced editor, it will meet two of the essential criteria for having your work assessed — it will be independent, and it will be done by people who have some understanding of the business of writing.

Assessments by friends and family fail both of these last two tests and should be avoided. Even if the family or friends are willing to tell you if they find fault with your work, unless you are very fortunate, they won't be professional editors. They may not even be fans of the genre your work sits within. Treat feedback from family or friends with a high degree of caution.

Writers' groups can also be a very useful source of 'beta readers'. Beta readers are often writers themselves. Their role, however, is to give you feedback as readers of your work. They should tell you how the story worked for them, whether the plot was engaging, whether any attempts at suspense worked for them, how they responded to the various characters, whether the love scene worked, whether some of your descriptions are overworked, and so on.

It may take some time before you can find some beta readers whose opinions or feedback you trust, but once you do tap into such a group, they can be invaluable. Once again, however, they are not a substitute for a professional editor. Having your work assessed by beta readers before you submit it to an editor, however, may enable you to identify and correct some of the issues before you spend money on a professional.

Spell-Checking and Grammar

While it is not uncommon to come across an error or two in a professionally published book, a book that contains more than just a rare few spelling or grammatical mistakes reeks of unprofessionalism. It sends a clear signal to the reader that the work has not been produced professionally and automatically begins to undermine their perception of its literary merits. While some readers may tolerate this, surveys indicate that most won't. Continued errors will distract their attention away from the merits of the story itself, ultimately leading to them deciding not to continue reading. This can be avoided with a bit of care.

Before you submit your work to a paid professional, you should do everything you reasonably can to identify and correct any spelling or basic grammar issues. Don't assume that you have eradicated all of these errors because you have used the spell-checker in the software program you used to draft your manuscript. While it is a good idea to use any spell-checking functions that are available in your software, be aware that these are far from foolproof. Nonetheless, you should use them as a matter of course, and remember to set the dictionary the program uses to the country of your choice. Microsoft Word, for example, allows you to set the spelling dictionary you require in its Preferences settings.

Another very useful software application to consider is Grammarly. I use this even if I have already developed the document and spell-checked it in Microsoft Word. Grammarly can be downloaded for free with basic functionality. An enhanced version of the application, with broader grammar checking functionality, is also available, though this incurs a monthly charge. Even the free version, however, is useful, and I have found it picks up a number of errors that are missed by the spelling and grammar checking in Microsoft Word.

Grammarly, of course, is just one program that offers this kind of functionality. There are many others. Have a look on the internet and see if there is a program that suits your purposes. At the end of the day, however, there is no substitute for the human eye. It is almost a certainty that in a lengthy manuscript there will be numerous spelling or grammatical mistakes that your software does not recognise. If you are using beta readers or critique groups, ask them to identify any spelling or grammatical errors they happen to notice.

It can be difficult for the author to identify many of these mistakes. When a person reads, they do not spell out every word in full in their mind. Quite often, the eye sees the basic shape of a word, and the brain then makes an assumption about what the word is without examining every letter. As the author of a document, you tend to already know what word or words you intended to use. As a result, this process speeds up for you when you are reading your own work. And it is for this same reason that even a trained editor can't guarantee to pick up every single spelling mistake. Almost every author complains at some point about the spelling mistakes that are still being identified, months, if not years, after their work has been published.

The best way to ensure as many mistakes as possible are picked up before your work goes to print is to check the document thoroughly yourself, use whatever software spelling and grammar checkers that are available, engage the services of an editor and then, for a final check, a proofreader. The proofreader specialises in identifying spelling and layout errors as the penultimate step prior to publishing.

Self-Editing

Finally, the work is ready to be handed to an editor. As I noted above, however, there will be cases where the author just cannot afford to have this work done by someone else. If this is the path you are following, here are a few things you absolutely must look out for. They range from 'big picture' issues such as point-of-view down to very detailed issues such as choice of font.

A number of these recommendations deal with setting up the appropriate 'Front Matter' pages. These include the Title Page, the Copyright Page, a Dedications Page (if you are having one), an Acknowledgements Page (if you are having one), a Table of Contents Page, and so on. Many of these pages need to be Facing Pages. That is, when you open up the book at any point, the Facing Page will be on the right. Establishing an Acknowledgements Page as a Facing Page, for example, may require you to insert a blank page between it and a previous Facing Page.

Similarly, 'End Matter' deals with any pages that exist after the end of the final chapter. An example might be an About the Author Page. This also should be on a Facing Page.

The downloadable Microsoft Word Manuscript Templates provided by Amazon KDP are available in two versions — one that is completely blank and one with sample content. The version with sample content makes setting up your manuscript in the correct manner, as well as dealing with a number of the recommendations below, a breeze.

To access these templates, do a Google search for 'KDP Help Centre Home'. Once you have accessed that page, type 'Paperback Manuscript Templates' in the search bar provided. This will take you to a page where you can download the templates. Before you choose a template, you will need to decide on the Trim Size for your book (refer to Step 3).

As editors often charge by the hour, completing the tasks below yourself can also reduce the cost, even if you intend to use a professional editor. Completing these tasks will also go a long way to ensuring that the final product looks professional and is easy to read.

- Read over your manuscript, keeping an eye out for consistency of point-of-view. If you don't have a good grasp on point-of-view, read up about it. Understanding it is an absolute must. You will find plenty of easy to follow advice about it on the internet. Keep an eye out for instances where you have inadvertently slipped from one point-of-view to another, and perhaps then back again. There is nothing wrong with having different points-of-view as your story progresses. As a general rule, however, each scene has only one point of view. Slipping between points-of-view at will is confusing to the reader. It is also an indication of work produced by an inexperienced writer and which has not been properly edited.

- Keep an eye out as you read over the text for obtuse words, where a simple word would do. The use of unusual and supposedly clever words is not a sign of a great writer. In fact, the opposite is probably more correct. Good writers keep their sentences crisp and clear.

- Also be on the lookout for unnecessary words, as in 'he clapped his hands'. What else would he clap with? Some suggest checking for every occurrence of 'very', then removing it and seeing if it detracts from the meaning of the sentence.

- For the file for publication of the print edition of your book, remove any hyperlinks. They will of course not be clickable in a printed book, but leaving them as hyperlinks may leave the font in a different colour which will then appear as a shade of grey when the book is printed in black and white. Leaving them as hyperlinks could also leave them underlined. For the file for the eBook edition of your publication, leaves the hyperlinks in, but check that they all link to the correct places.

- Do a search for troublesome words, particularly those that may be spelt correctly but are sometimes used incorrectly — words like 'its' or 'it's'; 'your' or 'you're'; 'affect' or 'effect'; 'in to' or 'into'; 'their', there' or 'they're'; 'then' or 'than'; and so on. If you're unsure which is the correct word to use, do a search on the internet for advice or check your grammar reference book.

- When reading over your work, keep an eye out for words that are repeated several times, either within one sentence or in a paragraph. See if some of these can be replaced with alternative words that have the same meaning.

- Check the font that you will be using for the text of your story, that is, for the content of the chapters in particular — deciding which font to use and which font size is a key consideration. For the print edition, this will in part be determined by the trim size of the book itself (see more on this in Step 3). The font to be used is an even more critical decision. Look at norms for your genre and do some research on the internet. Fancy fonts may look good to you on the screen, or even when you print them off at home, but can become very annoying, if not downright difficult, when a reader is reading a whole book. As a general rule, 'sans serif' fonts are difficult to read when used for an entire print book. The most commonly used fonts include Baskerville, Bembo, Garamond, Janson, Palatino and Times Roman. Choose your font carefully!

- Make sure that you have allowed for single spacing only between the full stop that concludes one sentence and the start of the next sentence in the same paragraph. Consider using the global replace function if you have used double spaces for the break between sentences extensively. A simple replace of 'full stop and one space' for 'full stop and two spaces' will fix this — but then check this hasn't upset any of your other formatting before proceeding further.

- Avoid the use of Tabs anywhere at all in your document. They invariably create problems when you convert your document into another format to upload for publishing.

- Do not put a Return at the end of a line. Only do this to start a new paragraph.

If you use the Amazon KDP downloadable Manuscript Template corresponding to the Trim Size you have chosen, the following points can be easily dealt with by using the Paragraph, and other Settings within the document. The template also provides sample 'Front Matter' and 'End Matter' pages with appropriate blank pages in place to ensure that relevant elements commence on Facing Pages.

- Consider the spacing you have allowed between paragraphs, as well as whether you have indented the first line of each paragraph. The standard for this may vary from genre to genre. You will notice that articles on websites often use a space between paragraphs rather than a 'first-line indent' to make such documents easier to read. This may also be the norm for some non-fiction books. Novels, however, tend to use a first-line indent instead. Typically, the first line should be indented somewhere between 1/4 and 1/2 inch. **Do not do this by using the tab key!** The Format Menu in Microsoft Word allows for formatting of paragraphs to provide for a first-line indent. Using this function in concert with Style settings, you can ensure consistency of approach throughout the whole manuscript. Other software applications will have similar functionality. It is a good idea to do this to every chapter before finalising your manuscript. You will be surprised how many rogue paragraph formats slip-in during the drafting stage with different settings from the norm. A sweep through at the end of your work can reset any of these and ensure consistency throughout your manuscript.

- At the same time that you are setting the first-line indent, decide upon and set a consistent approach to paragraph justification. The norms are either 'flush left', which tends to be used on the internet, or 'justified' (that is, both left and right sides of the document are aligned), which tends to be the standard for novels and most non-fiction books. Check what the norm is for your genre before deciding.

- Use page breaks between chapters.

- Make sure that each chapter begins in the same way. Use the same sized font for the chapter number or heading, place the chapter name or number in the same place and begin the text of the chapter the same number of lines down the page in every instance.

- Make sure your page numbers begin at one for the first page of the first chapter (rather than with the very first page of the book, which will most likely be the Title Page). At the same time, check that the page numbers follow on consecutively for each and every subsequent chapter. The general rule is that there should be no page numbers on the pages before the first chapter or after the end of the last chapter — with the possible exception of page numbering using roman numerals for a Foreword, Preface or Introduction of any length.

- Similarly, there should be no headers on the pages before the first chapter or after the last chapter. In fiction books, for the chapters themselves, the general rule is to have the author's name as the header on the left-hand page and the title of the book as the header on the right-hand page. This is called a 'running header' arrangement. In a non-fiction book, the book's title may appear in the header on the left-hand page and the chapter name in the header on the right-hand page. For fiction as well as non-fiction, there should be no header on the first page of a chapter. Microsoft Word provides functionality for all of this to occur. If you are not sure how to set this up in the software application you are using, Google it. There are bound to be instructions for this on the internet.

- Check that the alignment of the top and bottom lines of each page is consistent from page to page. When someone opens your book at any point, the top and bottom lines on both pages should align with each other.

- For the print edition of your book (be it a paperback or a hardback), ensure you have allowed for the correct 'Facing Pages'. Facing Pages are those on the right-hand side when you open a book at any point. Look at the norms for your genre before deciding these. The standard norms are as follows:
  - o The Title Page is usually the first facing page. Although it will be the first page in the file you upload for publishing, once your book is published, it will appear on the right-hand side when you open the cover, with the rear of the cover on your left-hand side. Every second page after this will also be a Facing Page.
  - o On the reverse of the Title Page is the Copyright Page. This will be on the left-hand side when the book is opened at that point and is therefore not on a Facing Page. Look at the norms for books published in your country for content for the Copyright Page and follow that. Generally, the Copyright Page content will be in a slightly smaller font to the rest of the publication, though this is not a hard and fast rule. As this page is where your ISBN should appear, you cannot complete your manuscript file for publication until you have obtained the ISBN for your work (refer to Step 5 for more on ISBNs).
  - o The next Facing Page may be a Dedication Page or an Acknowledgement Page. If your book will have both of these, place a blank page between them so that they both appear on Facing Pages. If you have a Quote Page, or a Map Page, they should also be on Facing Pages, with the appropriate blank pages in between to ensure this.
  - o Finally, Chapter One must begin on a Facing Page.
  - o Some authors start every subsequent chapter on a Facing Page as well, though this is not the norm.
  - o After the last chapter, you may include some more information, such as an About the Author page, or an Other Works page, and so on. These should probably also be on Facing Pages.
  - o For the eBook edition, having separate pages for matters such as Copyright details, Dedications, and the like still applies, with the exception that there should be no blank pages. The concept of a Facing Page has no meaning for an eBook.

Professional Editing

There are a number of reasons for paying the necessary dollars to have a professional editor review your manuscript.

- You can learn a lot from the experience by taking note of the corrections or adjustments they recommend and incorporating that learning into your next manuscript.
- It is probably the best way of ensuring the material you are going to present to the world is the very best that you can make it.
- As you gain experience and build up a portfolio of work, if you use a professional editor, particularly for your first book, you will be less likely to look back on it in horror as your knowledge and understanding of the craft of writing grows.

Don't have unrealistic expectations, however. A professional editor will not magically transform your work into a masterpiece. They will identify areas for improvement and pick up technical and other mistakes, but they won't rewrite your manuscript for you. It will be your decision what you do with the advice they provide.

A professional editor may complete a range of tasks, depending on what you engage them to do. The primary tasks may include some or all of the aspects of a manuscript assessment but will most likely also involve copy editing. Before you make a decision about whether to engage an editor, or which one to choose, make sure that there is clear agreement on exactly what they will do.

Shop around for an editor that you can work with. Your local or national writers' associations may offer advice or recommendations, or you may find colleagues who can recommend someone they have worked with previously. Paying an editor to assess your work and make recommendations for changes is likely to be one of your biggest expenses in preparing your work for publication. Make sure that you do your homework before you commit. Buried amongst the many excellent and reasonably priced professional editors is a whole industry waiting to prey on inexperienced authors, or authors who don't check what they are actually paying for. Once again, check with your local or national writers' groups or associations. They will usually have lists of properly credentialed service providers such as editors. More importantly, they also tend to have lists of service providers to avoid.

So, what is editing? To edit something means to revise it. The only purpose of revising something is to make it better. I have already outlined what is involved in a manuscript assessment earlier in this chapter. Copy editing is the process of checking written material for grammar, spelling, style, and punctuation issues.

A copy editor may also do a rewrite to fix problems with transitions, wordiness, jargon, and to ensure the style of the piece fits with the publication. Although many editors will have slightly different views on precisely what the process involves, the NY Book Editors website provides a useful and more detailed description. They advise that a copy editor:

- Checks for and corrects errors in grammar, spelling, syntax, and punctuation.
- Checks for technical consistency in spelling, capitalisation, font usage, numerals, hyphenation. For example, is it 'e-mail' on page 26 of your manuscript and 'email' on page 143? Or do you use both British and American English spelling variations interchangeably, such as 'favourite' versus 'favorite'?
- Checks for continuity errors and makes sure that all loose ends are tied.
- Checks for factually incorrect statements. This is a necessary part of the editing process for non-fiction manuscripts, such as historical pieces and memoirs. The editor must check if the facts in your manuscript are accurate and if the names and dates are correct.
- Checks for potential legal liability. The editor verifies that your manuscript does not libel others.
- Checks for inconsistency within the story. This includes character description, plot points, and setting. Does each character stay true to their own description throughout the story? Are there conflicting descriptions of a house, for example? Have you described the setting as 'a yellow brick home' on one page, but 'a weathered wooden cottage' elsewhere?

The copy editor's job, then, involves much more than just checking the grammar and the spelling. Editing and proofreading are separate tasks, although the terms are sometimes used interchangeably by people who don't know the difference.

A full edit of your manuscript, depending on its length and what tasks you and the editor have agreed upon, will probably cost between $1,000 and $2,000. In some cases, it may cost more than $2,000. It is an expensive but invaluable exercise that all authors should seriously consider.

———

STEP 3 — FORMATS, BOOK SIZE, PAPER TYPE, ETC.

Once your manuscript is completed and edited to your satisfaction, you will need to turn your attention to what size and type of book you want to publish. There is, however, no need to wait until this point. Some of these decisions can be made much earlier on in the process; they can also wait until you have finalised your content. The choice is up to you.

You should remember one very important point, however. Joanna Penn, a well-known author, blogger and experienced self-publisher, has made the following observation:

> "Writing is for the Author.
> Publishing is for the Book. Marketing is for the Reader."

This section of my guide to self-publishing is very much about the process of publishing. It is about what works best for the book. Avoid letting your own particular favourites detract from the professionalism of the final product. To put it simply, don't let your penchant for a particular type of fancy font, for example, interfere with a choice of what is best for your published book.

Book Size (Trim Size)

The following section applies to print versions of your book only, that is, to paperbacks and hardbacks; eBooks automatically resize to the dimensions of the electronic device they are being read on.

The first decision you will need to make is what size you want your printed book to be. By size, I mean the width and height of the cover, not the thickness. The latter, which equates to the width of the spine of the book, derives from, amongst other things, the length of your manuscript and the width and height of the cover.

As Amazon KDP is by far and away the leading publishing tool used by indie authors, I will concentrate on their processes and options for book size. While there are other companies that can publish your book for you, in my view they cannot match the ease of use and depth of support offered by Amazon KDP. The choice is yours, however, and you will find that the basic principles outlined here in respect of the Amazon process, also tend to apply to most of their competitors.

In the printing world, the dimensions of the front cover are referred to as the 'trim size'. This term refers to the dimensions of a document, such as the cover, after it has been printed and cut down to its desired width and height from a larger sheet, prior to any folding. Paper is trimmed to remove any excess around its perimeter or to separate pieces that have been printed as multiple images per sheet.

As you might expect, this is an old term which predates many of the modern printing processes. In the modern printing world, the cover for a printed book actually extends beyond the front cover to include the spine and the back cover. The term 'trim size', however, has stuck. It refers to the width and height of the front cover of your printed book.

You will see from the list below that there is a range of trim sizes for you to choose from. To find this information on the internet, simply Google 'Amazon KDP Print Options'.

For the publication you are reading, I chose a trim size of six inches by nine inches. That is, the front cover is six inches wide and nine inches high. I have used this same trim size in the past for my novels.

Amazon uses inches rather than centimetres as its standard for measurement but also includes the equivalent in centimetres in most cases.

Before deciding upon the trim size for your publication, have a look at other books in the genre. You will find their dimensions on Amazon's sale pages. Have a look at your local bookstore as well and note the variety of trim sizes that are sometimes used within the same genre.

At first appearance, you might think a choice of a larger trim size will result in a higher printing cost, but this is not necessarily so. On the one hand, a larger page would seem to require more paper and may lead, therefore, to a higher print cost. On the other hand, depending on the font size you choose, a larger page may provide space for more text than a smaller page, with a corresponding decrease in the overall number of pages.

Amazon KDP Trim sizes (without bleed) available:

5" x 8"	12.7 x 20.32 cm
5.06" x 7.91"	12.85 x 19.84 cm
5.25" x 8"	13.34 x 20.32 cm
5.5" x 8.5"	13.97 x 21.59 cm
6" x 9"	15.24 x 22.86 cm
6.14" x 9.21"	15.6 x 23.359 cm
6.69" x 9.61"	16.99 x 24.4 cm
7" x 10"	17.78 x 25.4 cm
7.44" x 9.69"	18.9 x 24.61 cm
7.5" x 9.25"	19.05 x 23.5 cm
8" x 10"	20.32 x 21.59 cm
8.5" x 11"	21.59 x 27.94 cm
8.25" x 68"	20.96 x 15.24 cm
8.25" x 8.25"	20.96 x 20.96 cm
8.27" x 11.69"	21 x 29.7 cm
8.5" x 8.5"	21.59 x 21.59 cm

Your decision regarding trim size will be a fundamental choice which will impact on a number of other steps along the path to publishing your book.

The trim size, for example, will determine the size of your book and allow work to begin on designing its cover. As the artwork will need to wrap around to include the spine and back cover, the full cover will not be able to be finalised until the width of the spine is known. This will not stop a cover designer, however, from having 95 percent of the work done, with the final touches simply awaiting the size of the spine.

The size of the spine is determined, once the trim size has been established, after you have finished formatting the contents of your book. Editorial changes, size of the font to be used, whether you will have a Dedication Page or an About the Author Page, and so on are just a few of the matters that need to be finalised before you can know how many pages will be required for your book. Amazon KDP (and other similar publishers) provide a tool which then determines the width of the spine for your book, the final ingredient that then allows your cover to be finalised.

Amazon KDP also provides Microsoft Word manuscript templates for each of the trim sizes available. These are handy tools for easy formatting of your book once you have decided upon the trim size (see Manuscript Format for Uploading to be Published below).

Font Size and Type

While you will have to choose your preferred font type for an eBook edition of your publication, you will only need to decide on font size for printed editions, that is, for paperbacks and hardbacks.

Printed Publications (Paperback or Hardback)

For your printed publication, your choices of what font type to use, along with what font size, are some of the most important decisions you will make. These choices will directly impact on the readability of the book for the reader.

While there are many fancy and attractive fonts available, they should be avoided. They may look good on screen, or on a greeting card or flyer, but having to read a whole book that has been printed in such a font is generally not a pleasant experience.

The general rule is that you **don't use a 'sans serif' font** for the print edition of your publication. This rule may be broken for some non-fiction books, but many of those also use serif fonts. Look at norms for your genre and do some research on the internet. The most commonly used fonts include Baskerville, Bembo, Garamond, Janson, Palatino and Times Roman. Choose your font carefully!

Font size will, at least in part, be determined by your choice of trim size. A very large font on a small page (or trim size) will not only look out of place; it will push your print cost per copy up considerably as it will push your page count much higher than it might otherwise have been. At the other extreme, a very small font size on a book with a large trim size will also look out of place, even if it does reduce the overall number of pages considerably. As a general rule, font sizes rarely stray outside of the 10 to 13 range, with the vast majority of printed books using a font size of 11 or 12. Other than the headings, the bulk of the text in this book is Garamond, size 11.

eBook Publication

When it comes to your eBook, you will find that sans serif fonts are sometimes used, though serif fonts are still the fonts of choice. Baskerville is frequently recommended as one of the best fonts for an eBook. Font size, however, is not a consideration with your eBook, as eBook devices and applications allow the reader to choose a font size that suits them.

Manuscript Format for Uploading to be Published

All publishers will require you to upload a file containing the formatted contents of your publication. A separate file will then need to be uploaded containing the artwork for your cover.

The file format required will vary depending on whether you are publishing the print edition of your book (the paperback or hardback edition) or your eBook edition.

Printed Publications (Paperback or Hardback)

For your print edition, Amazon KDP will accept a file containing the contents of your book (i.e. the final formatted manuscript with all of the pages and other required content) in the following formats:

- Microsoft Word (.doc or .docx)
- Adobe PDF (.pdf)
- Rich Text Format (.rtf).

The downloadable Microsoft Word Manuscript Templates for your manuscript that are provided by Amazon KDP are available in two versions — one that is blank and one with sample content. The version with sample content makes setting up your manuscript in the correct manner a breeze.

To access these templates, do a Google search for 'KDP Help Centre Home'. Once you have accessed that page, type 'Paperback Manuscript Templates' in the search bar provided. This will take you to a page where you can download the templates. Before you can choose a template, you will need to have decided on the Trim Size for your book (see above).

DO NOT at this stage upload your content to Amazon KDP. You have a few more tasks to complete before you are ready to do that. Getting your manuscript into one of the formats suitable for uploading, however, will simplify completing those additional tasks.

eBook Publication

For your eBook, Amazon KDP will accept a file containing the contents of your book (i.e. the final formatted manuscript with all of the pages and other required content) in the following formats:

- Kindle Create (.kpf)
- Microsoft Word (.doc or .docx)
- Adobe PDF (.pdf)
- Rich Text Format (.rtf)

- HTML
- MOBI
- EPUB
- Plain Text (.txt).

Kindle Create is probably the easiest of the above to use. Even if your manuscript is in one of the other formats, Kindle Create (which can be downloaded for free from Amazon KDP) will review the format, enable you to review it in an eReader similar to that used by people who purchase the eBook and will then create a file for uploading. Just Google 'Kindle Create' to find and download a free version of the program for use on either a Mac or a PC. The website provides a step-by-step tutorial if you need any further assistance, as well as answers to Frequently Asked Questions.

I used Vellum to format the eBook edition of this publication. While I find it a better tool to use than Kindle Create, it is a relatively expensive choice.

DO NOT at this stage upload your content to Amazon KDP. You have a few more tasks to complete before you are ready to do that. Getting your manuscript into one of the formats suitable for uploading, however, will simplify completing those additional tasks once we get to them.

Print Colour and Paper Type

For print editions of your manuscript, you will need to choose Print Colour and a Paper Type. Of course, there is no need for this with the eBook edition.

For Print Colour, you have a choice between Colour or Black and White. Most authors avoid colour unless it is absolutely essential. Colour print (e.g. for colour photographs, charts, diagrams, text, etc.) will push the print cost of your book up significantly. As a result, the price you charge will have to rise to cover those costs and allow for any profit you wish to make per sale. Unless you absolutely must have some items printed in colour, black and white will keep your print costs down and enable you to either set a lower price, or earn a healthy profit, or both.

Paper Type is a choice between Cream or White. Rather than choose what feels like a good idea to you, have a look at other books in your genre.

Choosing white paper for a novel, for example, sends a clear signal that your publication is self-published.

As a general rule, white paper is used for textbooks and many non-fiction publications, or any publication where there are colour images, as it allows for higher contrast with the colour of the image, chart or diagram. Most novels, however, are printed on cream paper.

As with so many other decisions, ultimately, the choice is yours.

Bleed Settings

The choices here are 'Bleed' or 'No Bleed'. Generally, you will set this to 'No Bleed'.

Bleed allows for some overrun of images or other elements which need to be printed right up to the edge of any of the pages. Bleed will ensure that such images extend just beyond the edge of the page so that when the page is trimmed after printing, there is no chance of a thin white line appearing between the printed image and the edge of the page.

If you still find this confusing, Google 'Amazon KDP Print Options' and have a look at the examples provided.

A novel or other story or text with no images will not need any Bleed. Even if images are included (I included some maps in my fantasy novel, *As Fire is to Gold: The Complete Chronicles of the Ilaroi*) you will still opt for 'No Bleed' unless the maps will be printed up against one or more of the edges of a page.

STEP 4 — GETTING A COVER

Print publication covers versus eBook covers

The cover requirements for print publications, such as paperbacks and hardbacks, differ from those for eBooks.

A print publication cover must be of sufficient size to allow for a front cover, the spine of the book, and a back cover — all in one combined document. A hardback cover differs from a paperback cover in that it requires additional artwork to either wrap around the side of the front and back covers (for a dust jacket cover), or to be folded over and pasted to the board which comprises the front and back covers (for a laminate cover).

An eBook has a front cover only (though some authors use the artwork from their print edition's back cover as a final image at the end of the interior of their eBook).

Print publication covers, therefore are more costly to produce than eBook covers. As the eBook cover can easily be derived (cropped) from the full print edition cover, it is not uncommon to design and build the print edition cover first, and then derive the eBook cover from that artwork.

Almost all cover designers who create print publication covers include an eBook cover in the package provided to the author.

The Importance of a Book's Cover

Everyone has heard of the saying: you can't judge a book by its cover. Most people will also agree that is true — you can't, or more accurately, *shouldn't* judge a book by its cover. Whatever the exterior looks like, be it a person, a book, or whatever, what lies within can be very different to the expectation created by its 'cover'.

What is also true, however, is that people invariably *do* judge books by their cover. Think of your own experience when you are in a bookshop. Putting aside the books you might look at because you know something about the author, or have read and liked some of their other work, what else would you look at? Would you take down every single other book and examine it to see if you like it?

No. Of course not. Putting aside some familiarity with the author's work, the appeal of the cover tends to be one of the strongest influences as to what other books we might decide to take a closer look at. That's why, when bookshops are promoting certain books, they display them so that their cover faces the customers.

In fact, surveys of customers have firmly established that the top four things which influence people to consider any given book run as follows, from the most influential down:

- The author's reputation or what they already know about the author.
- The book's cover.
- The 'blurb' on the back of the cover.
- Good reviews from other readers or from authors of note.

The same applies if the book is being marketed on the internet. The main difference here is that the seller doesn't have to overcome the fact that, for the majority of books on their 'shelves', only the book's spine will be visible. On the internet, all books have their front cover on display. An equivalent to the 'blurb', which in a physical bookshelf will only have been accessible by picking the book up and turning it around, will be displayed to the side or below the cover, as will any reviews or recommendations.

What this tells us is that, if you want to sell your book once it is published and for sale in a bookshop, or on Amazon or some other online bookseller's website, the cover is the primary thing that will either catch a potential customer's attention — or not. Once a potential customer passes your book by, in all likelihood, that is it. They won't stop to read the blurb or the reviews. They'll move on to one of the hundreds if not thousands of other books available.

Can you compete with the big publishing companies' covers?

Fortunately, there is no reason why a self-published author can't have a cover that is as good as, if not better than, some of the covers paid for by the big publishers. There is also no reason why a self-published author's book, cover included, can't be almost indistinguishable from a traditionally published book. The trick is to take a bit of care and invest a bit of time, and perhaps some money too, to give your book all of the features of a traditionally published book.

The cover is the first issue to be dealt with in this regard, and the only one that will potentially cost you some dollars.

There are hundreds if not thousands of service providers on the internet who will work with you to design a cover for your book according to your specifications. This can cost you as little as $50 and as much as $1,000 to $1,500. If your outlay is in the several hundreds of dollars or higher, there is a very good chance that you can acquire a better cover than many of those produced by the big publishers.

There are some great cover designers out there. For around $500 and upwards, and certainly, as you get up around the $700 to $1,000 mark, you can engage an adept cover designer, who knows their trade and has the skills to produce stunning covers.

They will work to your specifications, as you know your book. Your cover designer is not going to read your story. The good ones will want to know what it is about, what the mood of the book is, and, most importantly, whether you have any particular vision for its cover. This is where you need to do your homework.

Think about who your target audience is — a cover that appeals to a young adult reader will probably be very different to one that attracts a mature-aged reader. Look at other books in your genre. Keep a copy of several of the covers you like. When you engage a cover designer, apart from getting you to tell them what your book is about, they will invariably ask you to send them pictures of, or links to, some of the covers you like.

They may also ask whether you have any particular ideas about what you want to have displayed on the cover. In my case, for my fantasy novel, *As Fire is to Gold*, I had a very specific idea of what I wanted. I preferred an illustrated cover as I felt that better suited an epic fantasy novel. I was conscious that my central character was a young female and, as the story was basically about one long chase, I wanted the cover to reflect both of those elements.

I discussed all of that with the designer I chose, and he came back with some rough sketches until I was happy with the direction it was going. I live in New Zealand, and he lives in New Mexico. That wasn't a problem. We skyped for about half an hour until he was sure he understood the look and the feel I was hoping to see on my cover. I couldn't have been happier with the result.

There were a number of other things he needed before the cover could be finalised (more about those below), but they were easy to add once the underlying artwork was sorted out.

Before you engage a cover designer, check what you will get for your money. A comprehensive cover package will generally include:

- a 'print ready file' (probably a PDF or a JPEG) which is a full wrap-around cover for your print paperback (and/or hardcover if that is where you are going)
- three or more initial design concepts for you to choose from before the cover designer puts the work into finalising the cover based on the design you prefer
- a separate cover file for your eBook (as the eBook only requires a front cover)
- perhaps a 3D mock-up of your cover, or some other cover image suitable for use on your author website, if you have one (refer to Chapter 8 for more about Author Websites).

You should also check whether your cover designer is prepared to provide you with the original files, which will most likely be in Photoshop. If they don't, then any time you want to make a change to the cover, for whatever reason, you will need to go back to them to make those changes.

Some designers will hand over the original files at no additional cost if asked. Some will provide them for a small additional fee — perhaps an extra $50 or so. Some will not hand over the original files but will make any future amendments for a small and very reasonable fee. Only you can decide what will work best for you.

When you self-publish through Amazon KDP, after your book is published you can still make changes to either the content or the cover any time you want to. You can't change the title or your author name; they are set in stone. Pretty much everything else, however, can be changed whenever you deem it necessary. There is no charge for such changes.

In my case, I have made some changes to the blurb on the back cover since my novel was originally published. Although my Photoshop skills are rudimentary, because I asked my cover designer for the original files (which he then provided at no further cost) I was able to make the changes to my back-cover blurb and upload the new cover with a minimum of fuss.

Trim Size

Before your cover designer, whoever that is, can begin work on your cover they will need to know the trim size you have opted for (refer to Step 3), as this will determine the size of the 'canvas' they have to work with.

Blurb

You will also need to write a 'blurb' for the back cover of your book. Do some research on blurbs other authors in your genre have used. As noted above, your cover designer will be able to get started without the blurb having been finalised. They will, however, need the final content of your blurb before the cover can be finished.

You will quickly find that **a blurb is not simply a synopsis of your story**. Its role is to entice the customer. It is a marketing tool. It generally hints at or reveals the overall premise of your book without giving away too many specifics. It should attract a potential customer's interest and make them think: 'this sounds like the type of book I would like to read'.

Note what I said above about the three most important things that influence a customer's decision to purchase a book. The blurb came in at number three, right after the author's reputation and the front cover.

Once you've attracted the customer's interest with your front cover, the blurb is your big chance to cement that interest and convince them to buy the book. The vast majority of book sales occur on the internet these days, so there may be little if any opportunity for the potential buyer to open your book up and read a few paragraphs. **The blurb is important, so spend some time crafting it to get it right**.

Keep it relatively brief and to the point as well. It has to fit on to the back cover, along with the book's barcode, perhaps a publishing imprint, any review snippets or testimonials, and so on.

Run your draft past some people and test their reaction. There are numerous Facebook groups where you can do just that. Once again, have a look on the internet as well. There are plenty of articles on how to write a great blurb.

Reviews or Awards

You are probably unlikely to have any good reviews of your book before it is published. If you do, however, consider putting a quote from one or more of them on the cover — probably on the back cover. Similarly, if you've won any awards of significance, say so on the cover. 'Best Short Story' in your local town's writers' group's competition probably won't cut it, but if you've won something significant, tell your customers.

Don't forget that you can update your cover any time you want to, at no cost. If and when you do get some good reviews, consider updating the cover to reflect them. Good reviews definitely help sell books.

Publishing Imprint

Although it is diminishing at a rapid rate now, there is still an aversion amongst some customers to self-published books. One way to overcome this is to make your book almost indistinguishable from one that has been produced by one of the major publishing houses. An important step in achieving this is to publish it under your own 'Publishing Imprint'.

Have a look at a book from your bookshelf that you know was published by a traditional publisher. Do you see a logo at the bottom (or perhaps the top) of the spine? There might also be another variation on the back cover. This is the publishing imprint — the publishing house's 'branding'.

The absence of any such logos (they don't have to be on the spine *and* the back cover, but are almost always on the spine at least) is almost a sure sign that a book is self-published. Inclusion of such logos is not, however, a guarantee that the work is published by a publishing house. More and more self-published authors are putting their own publishing imprint on their books, and even naming their publishing imprint on the Copyright Page as well.

This is not hard to do. I had a local designer work up some images for a publishing imprint for my books. It cost me $120 for several images — square images for the spine and a larger one for the back cover, both in black on white as well as white on black. By having both colour variations, one or other of the images should work regardless of the colour used on my covers. When I engaged a cover designer, I sent him the publishing imprint images and asked him to include them in his design. There were no additional charges for him to do that.

I went a step further. My publishing imprint is named Serotine Press Australia. It has its own website (at this stage only a single page) at https://serotinepress.com.au. I publish on Amazon under that imprint, but also of course under my own name as the author. I also purchase my ISBNs under that name. It has no impact on my access to royalties and the like. Some of the mail I receive about my book from Amazon and others goes to Serotine Press Australia, but that is my own address anyway.

Its purpose is to help complete the perception that my books are professionally published — which I wholeheartedly believe they are.

Some bloggers criticise this approach. They claim that it is misleading, that it creates the impression a book has had all the vetting processes applied to it, such as professional editing and proofreading, that apply to books published through a traditional publishing house.

As one commentator has responded — hogwash! Many local businesses and tiny operations run by individuals with no apparent business skills or qualifications put logos on their storefront or on their stationery, or use a professional sounding business name or livery. This is part of running a business — presenting yourself as professionally as you reasonably can.

Give serious consideration to doing this. As I have noted above, the absence of a publishing imprint on the cover is almost a sure sign that a book is self-published. That may not matter to you, but if it does, it is easy to rectify.

Apply some creative thinking to the process of naming and designing your imprint. Do some internet searches to make sure that some other business is not already using the name. Check domain names for the same purpose. Consider taking the additional step of buying the domain name, and even registering the business name, if your funds go that far. Neither of those processes is very expensive. Don't include your author name in the imprint name. Have some fun with it.

ISBNs

You won't need to know your book's ISBN number in order to finalise your cover. You will need to know it in order to finalise your manuscript file, however, as the book's ISBN number should appear on the book's Copyright Page. Step 5 explains more about ISBNs.

Spine width

You won't be able to determine the spine width for your book until you have locked down the text and formatted all of the pages. Completing that task will tell you how many physical pages there will be in your book. This is not the number of pages for the chapters. Rather it is all of the pages, from the Title Page right through to the very last leaf. Once that number is known, download Amazon KDP's 'Paperback file setup calculator, and that will help you establish the width of the spine for your book. Provide this information to your cover designer so that he can finalise your cover.

You can find the paperback file setup calculator by going to Amazon KDP at https://kdp.amazon.com/. Then go to the Help page and type in 'Paperback cover resources'. The Paperback Cover Resources page will provide a link for you to download the calculator.

Can you get a good cover for little or no cost?

I guess the key word here is 'good'. Beauty, or good cover design, is in the eye of the beholder. You can certainly get a cover for a very small outlay — in some cases, less than $100. Whether these are 'good' covers is arguable.

Have a look on the internet, or go to Facebook groups like Book Design Cover Marketplace. Make sure that you are getting a full cover (a front cover, spine and back cover) if you are planning a print edition of your book and not just an eBook.

If you are thinking of going down this path, remember what I said above about the impact of good — or bad — cover design. It can make or break your chances of success in terms of sales. Good cover designers charge for their skill, time and effort. Adequate cover designers tend to charge less.

We all have budgets to work with, however. You may long to spend the money on a great cover, but it just may not be an option given the funds that are available to you. I guess the best recommendation I can make is that you get the best cover you can afford.

The following are just a few of the lower-cost cover design providers available on the internet. I can offer no guarantees on the quality of their work or of their other bona fides. As with all things of this nature, check what you will actually receive and what further costs might be involved should you wish to make additional minor changes down the track. In short, do your homework before you commit to any expenditure:

- Bookcoverexpress.com
- Coverdesignstudio.com
- Bookdesigntemplates.com
- Bookscovered.co.uk
- 17studiobookdesign.com
- Reedsy.com
- Damonza.com
- TheBookcoverdesigner.com.

Can you design your own cover?

You certainly can design your own cover for zero financial outlay. It's your choice if that is the way you choose to go. My recommendation, if this is the path you are considering, is that you still do your homework and look at what works for covers in your genre. Try to emulate the look and feel of the better covers if you can. Look at the types of images that are commonly used in your genre. Look at how different covers treat the comparative size and placement of the book's title and the author's name. Look at the length of a typical back-cover blurb, and the types of things that go into a blurb.

Websites such as canva.com enable you to design your own cover, choosing from a range of styles and templates provided, at no cost to you. Though this is one of the most prominent sites, there are a number of others offering similar services. Do some Googling and see what you can discover. Sites such as Unsplash, with their supply of stock photos available for use at no cost, can also be a useful source of images to make your cover just that little bit different from the rest. Once again, Google and see what you can find.

Whatever you do, put some time into making it look as professional as you can. Remember, people do judge a book by its cover.

———

STEP 5 — THE ISBN

What is an ISBN and why must you have one?

An ISBN is an International Standard Book Number. ISBNs were 10 digits in length up to the end of December 2006, but from 1 January 2007 they now always consist of 13 digits. ISBNs are calculated using a specific mathematical formula and include a check digit to validate the number.

Each ISBN consists of five elements, with each section being separated by spaces or hyphens. Three of the five elements may be of varying length. They include:

- A prefix element, always three digits in length – currently this can only be either 978 or 979.
- A registration group element, between one and five digits in length, identifying the particular country, geographical region, or language area participating in the ISBN system.
- A registrant element, up to seven digits in length, identifying the particular publisher or imprint.

- A publication element, up to 6 digits in length, identifying the particular edition and format of a specific title.
- A check digit or final single digit that mathematically validates the rest of the number. It is calculated using a Modulus 10 system with alternate weights of one and three.

An ISBN is essentially a product identifier used by publishers, booksellers, libraries, internet retailers and other supply chain participants for ordering, listing, sales records and stock control purposes. In a nutshell, the ISBN identifies the registrant as well as the specific title, edition and format.

When you purchase an ISBN, you will need to provide some information about your book, such as the title, the publisher's details (that may be you), the author name, and the like, which will go into an international database which can be accessed by publishers, booksellers, libraries and other similar groups. The amount of information required can seem overwhelming at first, but the actual number of fields that are mandatory is, in fact, very small.

You must have an ISBN for the paperback or hardback editions of your book. If you are publishing a paperback edition and a hardback edition, you will need separate ISBNs for each of these editions. See below for advice about Amazon and other companies' offers of a free ISBN.

Amazon doesn't require an ISBN for an eBook, but many authors use one anyway. If you do that, it cannot be one you have already used elsewhere, such as for the paperback or hardback editions. If you go on to publish your eBook through Smashwords and Draft2Digital, as well as Amazon, these companies will require that your eBook have an ISBN and it must be a different one to one you might have used with Amazon. See more about ISBNs for eBooks in Step 6.

Should you use the free ISBN offered by Amazon KDP and others?

Amazon KDP offers to supply you with a free ISBN for your paperback publication. If you take up this offer, your book will be published under Amazon KDP's imprint, and you cannot publish that version anywhere else. This may be fine for you. You may have no desire to publish the print edition of your publication elsewhere. You may also be content with it being published under Amazon KDP's publishing imprint.

In my case, I wanted to publish my novel through IngramSpark as well as Amazon KDP (more about this in Chapter 6). I also took the view that publishing under the Amazon KDP publishing imprint would send a clear signal to the marketplace that mine was a self-published novel. I wanted to use my own publishing imprint. I also wanted to very clearly retain all rights to where and with whom I published my work. As I would be publishing under my own Australian publishing imprint, a block of ten ISBNs, would cost me only A$8.80 per ISBN. I decided to use my own ISBN.

For your book, the choice is yours. What you decide will depend on your own circumstances, views, and goals. Be careful, however. Initially, you may decide that you are fine with the limitations that come with a free ISBN from Amazon KDP, or some other publisher, but then change your mind down the track as you discover more about the publishing world or as your goals change. Using your own ISBN right from the start ensures that you will have complete freedom to consider alternative paths should you wish to later on.

Where can you get ISBNs and what do they cost?

In some countries, ISBNs are available free of charge; in others, you will have to pay a small fee. If you are paying for your ISBN, consider taking up one of the offers for a block of ISBNs at a greatly reduced fee. In the case of my novel, I ended up needing six, with separate ISBNs for:

- a paperback edition
- a hardback edition
- a large print edition
- an eBook edition with Amazon
- an eBook edition with Draft2Digital
- an eBook edition with Smashwords.

It could be the case that I was being needlessly cautious in some, if not all, of the above instances. After all, in every instance, I had the opportunity to go with a free ISBN provided by the service provider. At a cost to me of

A$8.80 per ISBN, that didn't worry me.

Remember to allow for the time it takes to have an ISBN allocated to you in your country. In some countries, you can log on to the internet and get your ISBN as soon as you complete the required information. In others, it may take anywhere from a few days to up to a week or more.

- In the **USA**, ISBNs are supplied by Bowker. Refer to their website at https://www.isbn.org/. One ISBN will cost you US$125. A block of 10 will cost US$295.
- In the **United Kingdom**, ISBNs are available from Nielsen. Refer to the website at https://www.bl.uk/help/get-an-isbn-or-issn-for-your-publication. One ISBN will cost you £99. A block of 10 will cost £179.
- In **Canada**, ISBNs are available for free from Library and Archives Canada. Refer to their website at http://www.bac-lac.gc.ca/eng/services/isbn-canada/Pages/isbn-canada.aspx.
- In **Australia**, ISBNs are available from Thorpe Bowker. Their website is at www.bowker.com/products/ISBN-AU.html. One ISBN will cost you A$44. You can purchase 10 for A$88.
- In **New Zealand**, ISBNs are allocated by the National Library of New Zealand. The library does not charge you for an ISBN.
- For **all other countries**, check for advice on the internet about how to get an ISBN in your country.

Should you have an ISBN for your eBook?

This will be discussed further under Step 6. The short answer is that you don't have to have an ISBN for your eBook when it is published through Amazon KDP. Smashwords and Draft2Digital will require an ISBN if you publish through them. They do, however, offer free ISBNs, albeit with some limitations to your rights.

In my case, I used my own ISBNs for all of my publications, including any eBook publications produced through Amazon KDP.

STEP 6 — REGISTERING WITH AMAZON KDP

To register with Amazon KDP (go to https://kdp.amazon.com/) you will need an Amazon logon. Do this under the email address you intend to use for work on your publication. You may already have an Amazon logon — that is fine. Just remember that whatever email address you use will be the one that all future emails about your publication will be sent to by Amazon.

Apart from the fact that you have to register with Amazon KDP to use their publishing function, registering will also get you on to their email list for notifications about upcoming webinars that they run, along with other updates about their service. The webinars are actually quite good, and I would recommend you consider participating in some of them. They are free!

Once you register, you will gain access to a number of menus, the most important of which is the Bookshelf. There is no charge for registering. In fact, there is no charge for publishing with Amazon KDP. Amazon simply takes a percentage of any royalties earned from sales of your published book through their distribution network and then distribute the remainder to you. The royalties percentage payable to you far exceeds percentages paid by any of the traditional publishers.

The Bookshelf operates much like a Control Panel. This is where you input information such as the title and author's name, choose keywords that will enable potential customers to find your book on Amazon's website, upload your final manuscript and your cover, decide on pricing and distribution options, and so on.

Input of all of the information occurs over three sub-pages — a Paperback (or eBook) Details Page, a Paperback (or eBook) Content Page and a Paperback (or eBook) Rights & Pricing Page. All of the inputs required will be discussed below to help you determine the best ways to respond.

Before we deal with these in greater detail, you will notice a number of other menu items available at the top of the Bookshelf page. 'Reports' will provide you with a range of information regarding sales and royalties paid once your book is published. You can access these as often as you like; you don't have to wait for Amazon to decide to send you a report. 'Community' will give you access to Discussion Boards where other users discuss items of interest. 'KDP Select' pertains specifically to your eBooks. Choosing to access KDP Select is optional. While the option has some useful benefits, it also comes with consequences. You should check what the benefits and disadvantages are before making the choice. Refer to Step 9 for more information about KDP Select.

Perhaps one of the most useful links on this page is the 'Help' option in the top right corner. One of Amazon KDP's big advantages is their wide range of Help advice, along with its ease of use. This includes instructions or explanations, internet-based seminars and even short videos on almost every aspect of their service. You will almost certainly access some of this information at some stage during the publishing process. The KDP University link on the right-hand side of the KDP Help Center Home page gives you quick access to some of the more important resources.

The Bookshelf

The first thing you will notice about your Bookshelf is that it is empty! When you do decide to create an entry, you will need to create separate items for either or both of an eBook and a paperback option. You don't have to have both. You could opt just for an eBook edition only, or a paperback edition only, or you can take the usual approach and have both.

I always go with both. I love printed books, but the vast bulk of sales these days comes from eBooks, whether you personally happen to like them or not. I always start with the paperback edition, as the eBook edition tends to require a cut-down of the information you have already compiled for the paperback.

It is also worth noting that you don't have to be ready to publish before you can create an item on your Bookshelf. You can create an item for a book you are working with, providing a bare minimum of details and then add more information as and when you are ready. I like to do this as it helps motivate me to get on with the task of completing my manuscript. The choice is yours whether you do the same.

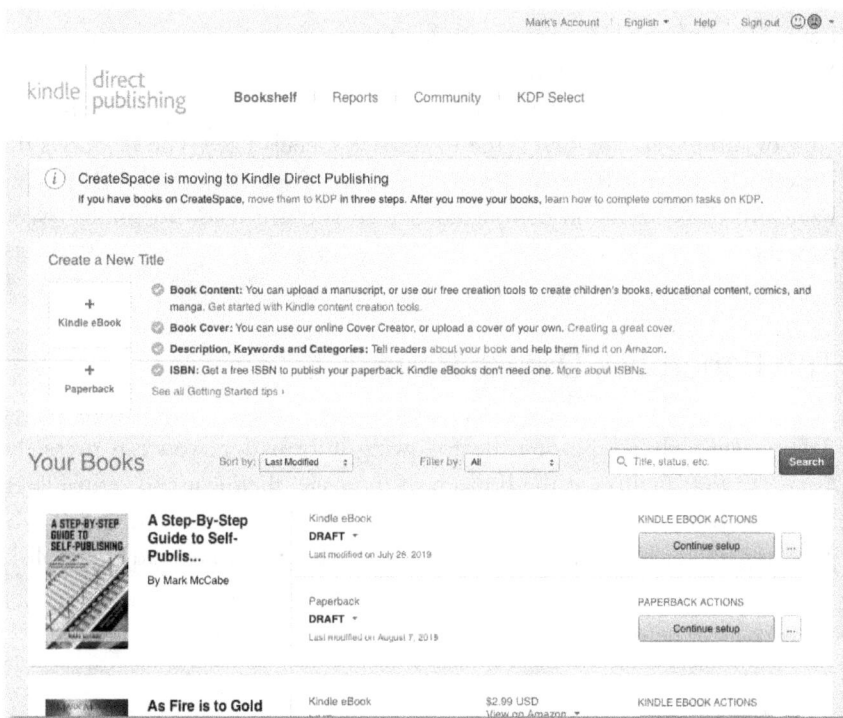

You will also see from the example above, that your Bookshelf entry will display a mock-up of your cover once you have input a graphic for your eBook cover. Once again, this need not be your final choice of cover art. One of the great things about the Bookshelf is that you can make changes to it at any time up to, and in fact after, publication occurs, at no cost to you.

Over the following pages, I will take you for the requirements for creating entries for both a paperback edition of your manuscript and for an eBook edition. Let's start with a paperback; then I will walk you through the same process for an eBook, noting the slight differences between the requirements for an eBook when compared to a paperback. While some may find the eBook information repetitive, please bear with me, as some readers may not want to publish a paperback and may, therefore, skip that section and go straight to the eBook section.

Creating a Paperback Entry on the Bookshelf

Let's start with the information required to get your Bookshelf entry going. You do this by clicking on the plus sign for a Paperback under Create a New Title. Once you do this, you will immediately be taken to a page with three tabs, or sub-pages. The first is the Paperback Details Page. The second is the Paperback Content Page, and the third is the Paperback Rights & Pricing Page. All three must be completed before you are ready to publish your paperback.

The Paperback Details Page

At any stage while inputting the following information, you can press the 'Save as Draft' button at the bottom of the page, then exit and return later. Similarly, you can 'Save and Continue', which will take you to the next sub-page, yet still make changes right up until you decide you are ready to publish.

You will not be committed until you press the 'Publish Your Paperback Book' button on the third sub-page, Paperback Rights and Pricing.

Language

Select the language your book is written in from the dropdown menu.

Book Title

This is a very important field, for a number of reasons, the primary one being that **once your book is published, the title cannot be changed**, it is set in stone. You can change it as often as you like before you decide to publish your book, but not after that step has been taken.

Amazon also advises that books are linked automatically if the author name and book title of both formats (eBook and paperback) match exactly. They advise that during the publishing process, KDP tries to match book details like title and author name to other editions available in the Amazon catalogue. As linking these formats provides the ideal browsing experience for customers, they encourage you to make sure the title and author name you entered for your eBook and paperback match exactly.

This is advice that you should follow. Having your eBook and your paperback or other editions linked is a good thing from a marketing point of view. It is hard to see how having different titles for what is essentially the same book can work to your advantage. It would, however, confuse your customers no end.

If you acquired your own ISBN, the book title entered here must match the book title you entered when registering your ISBN.

The Subtitle field is optional.

Series

If your book is part of a series, you can put the series name here. This can be useful. I first published my novel in two parts: *As Fire is to Gold*, which was Book 1 of the Chronicles of the Ilaroi, and *When All the Leaves Have Fallen*, which was Book 2 of the Chronicles of the Ilaroi.

I used the Series field on the Bookshelf to indicate the name of the series — *Chronicles of the Ilaroi*. For the first book, *As Fire is to Gold*, I entered the number '1' in the Series Number field. *When All the Leaves Have Fallen* was, of course, number '2'.

One of the advantages of this was that, once both books had been published, I was able to ask Amazon to create a Series Page on their website. You can see what this looks like in the image on the next page (Note: All the images in this book are printed in black and white. The actual screen image is, of course, in colour).

As a side note, I later combined these two books into one volume by creating a third publication. As I liked the title of Book 1, but a new publication had to have a different name, I titled it, *As Fire is to Gold: The Complete Chronicles of the Ilaroi.*

This was not an ideal solution. It would have been better if I had thought this through before I published the first two books. You learn from your experiences.

Edition Number

This field is relevant if you are publishing a book which you can expect might have subsequent further editions. I expect to update the book you are reading, for example, as aspects of the self-publishing process change or improve over time. Knowing this, I have put the number '1' in the Edition Number field.

Author

Warning: This field may seem fairly innocuous, but you should treat it carefully.

Once the publishing process is complete, the way you have input your author name here will be the way it is for this book forevermore. If I put 'Mr Mark McCabe', for example, then that would be my author name on the Amazon or any other distributor's sales page. Similarly, if I put 'Mark A. McCabe', that would be the name that would appear. Just as with your book title, whatever option you choose for **your author name in this field cannot be changed after publication**.

If you subsequently decide you prefer just plain 'Mark McCabe', then any books subsequently published under that name will appear separately to those published by 'Mark A. McCabe' or 'Mr Mark McCabe'. Think this through carefully before you make your choice.

Your choice of how you display your author name can work to your advantage if you want it to. Joanna Penn, a well-known author and blogger, publishes non-fiction books as 'Joanna Penn' and supernatural thrillers as 'J.F.Penn'. As she says, she is not trying to hide her identity by having two different names for publication, she simply has different audiences and therefore different profiles and different marketing for the two categories of work she produces.

In a similar vein, there is nothing to stop you from publishing under a 'pen name'. Your Amazon account will be under your real name, but your book will be linked to your author or 'pen' name. You will need to take a few additional steps when setting up your Amazon Author Page so that it is properly linked to your account, but this is not difficult. I will walk you through how to do that in Chapter 7.

Contributors

This is where you can add any other people involved in the creation of your book other than yourself as the author. Amazon KDP advises that this could include editors, illustrators, translators, and anyone else you want to give credit to, as long as they worked on the book. You can enter multiple contributors.

It is your choice whether you add other contributors. I suspect that most authors only add those who have contributed content, such as illustrators and the like.

Make sure that if you are going to add other persons, you have checked that they are happy for you to do so. It wouldn't hurt for them to put that in writing (an email is considered to be 'in writing').

Description

This is another very important field. The contents of this field will appear on your Amazon sales page. If a potential customer looking for a book to buy online likes the look of your cover, this description is invariably what they will look at next to help them make their decision whether to buy it or not.

You need to put some time and effort into getting this just right. Just as for the blurb on your cover, do some Googling and have a look at some of the advice on the internet about how to write a good description. Perhaps start with this page — https://blog.reedsy.com/book-description/ — and then see what else you can find. Don't forget there is a text limit of 3,988 characters for your description. Don't write War and Peace!

You can change the contents of this field after your book is published, and you will probably find yourself doing just that, tinkering with it and fine-tuning it, or simply refreshing it with a new look every so often. You do, nonetheless, want a good description on your sales page when your book is first published.

When I am first creating my book entry on my Bookshelf, I tend to simply put 'Expand later' here, and then work on my description offline until I am ready to complete this field properly prior to publication.

One bugbear is that you cannot format the text here. Although you will be able to directly replace it, along with a little bit of formatting, through your Amazon Author Page after publication (more about this in Chapter 7), every time you update this page on your Bookshelf subsequent to publication, the contents of this field will overwrite anything you have entered through the Amazon Author Page. This can be very annoying, particularly if you forget that will happen and only realise sometime later that your carefully crafted description has been over-written by an older version

Kindlepreneur.com provide an excellent free online book description generator tool which will format your book description for you. You still have to come up with the content, but it then takes your description, along with your choice of formatting, and generates a coded version which you can copy and paste into the Description field so that it displays on Amazon's Sales Page exactly how you intended it to. I have bookmarked this internet page in my browser and use it regularly.

Publishing Rights

If you wrote your manuscript, you own the copyright and hold the necessary publishing rights. If that is the case, you will click on the first radio button in this field. Click on the links provided in this field if you are in any doubt.

Keywords

This is yet another important field. It is optional, but overlook it at your peril. Put simply, Keywords are words that Amazon's behind-the-scenes software look for when a potential buyer is searching for a book. Amazon uses any keywords that appear in their search text to direct them to a page or pages (i.e. to books) that match their declared interest. Getting your keywords right, then, is of critical importance in drawing potential customers to your book page.

Once again, the best way to tackle this is to do a bit of research on the internet. Amazon KDP offers some help in this regard. Go to KDP's Help Topics and do a search for 'Choose Browse Categories'. Once you find that page, scroll down until you reach the sub-heading, 'Categories with keyword requirements'. Click on your genre, and you will find a useful list of keywords to get you started.

Don't stop there, however. There is an immense amount of useful information out there to help you. Do a Google search for keywords relevant to your specific genre.

As you can add to or amend this field subsequent to publication, one useful approach after your book has been published is to run a simple advertisement for a very small expenditure (perhaps $20 to $30, or even less) through Amazon to test a number of keywords and see which are the most successful in drawing buyers to your book page. You will find more about this in Chapter 9.

Using a good keyword, or keywords, won't guarantee sales, but it can ensure potential customers at least find your book. Whether they then buy it is going to depend on all those other issues we have already discussed — the cover, the blurb, the description, etc. None of these factors can come into play, however, until you can get a potential buyer to your book page.

Amazon KDP allow you to use up to seven keywords.

Categories

Categories, fortunately, are much simpler to identify then Keywords. Simply click on the 'Choose categories' button and follow the most likely path for your book, given its content and genre. Think of it as being similar to the categories a physical bookstore uses to separate different types of books. Most bookstores will have a Crime / Mystery section, a Sci-Fi and Fantasy section, perhaps a Romance section, a Travel section, and so on. Categories work in the same way, though they drill down further within those very broad categories. Amazon KDP allow you to choose up to two categories.

You can also opt to make your book a 'large print' book by clicking on the checkbox here. This will not be in addition to a normal print edition. Checking this box will make this edition a Large Print edition. If you do this, you will need to increase the font size of your manuscript accordingly, probably up to size 16 at least.

I would not recommend doing this with your first publication, though you may want to consider adding a large print edition down the track. Given that there is no charge for publishing with a print-on-demand service such as Amazon KDP, the only costs to you will be any fee you might have to pay for another ISBN and any money you might spend on adding a Large Print 'sticker' to your cover, or even on making the cover bigger as you will probably need to opt for a larger Trim Size book for a Large Print edition.

Some authors swear by Large Print editions. One author claims that, for one of her books, the distribution of sales in the first year was:

- 52% eBook
- 12% Standard Paperback
- 36% Large Print.

The book she was referring to was a romance novel targeted at mature readers. I cannot say whether the genre or target audience were influencing factors in the above result, though I suspect that is the case.

Adult Content

Indicate whether any of the contents of your book are inappropriate for children under 18 years of age.

As noted above, at any stage while inputting the above information, you can press the 'Save as Draft' button at the bottom of the page, then exit and return later. Similarly, you can 'Save and Continue', yet still make changes right up until you decide you are ready to publish.

You will not be committed until you press the 'Publish Your Paperback Book' button on the third page, Paperback Rights and Pricing.

The Paperback Content Page

Once again, at any stage while inputting the following information, you can press the 'Save as Draft' button at the bottom of the page, then exit and return later. Similarly, you can 'Save and Continue', yet still make changes right up until you decide you are ready to publish.

You will not be committed until you press the 'Publish Your Paperback Book' button on the third page, Paperback Rights and Pricing.

Print ISBN

All print publications, including paperbacks, must have an ISBN. You can either use a free ISBN supplied by Amazon KDP or provide your own.

Step 5 covers the requirements associated with ISBNs in more detail. Go back and read those if you haven't already done so, particularly my advice under the subheading, 'Should you use the free ISBN offered by Amazon KDP and others?'. Many authors opt for Amazon KDP's offer of a free ISBN. I always use my own, as I want to be absolutely sure that I retain all the rights to my book. The choice is yours.

If you do decide to use your own ISBN, and if you acquired that ISBN under the name of your own, or some other, publishing imprint, you must enter the name of that publishing imprint in the space provided. Amazon KDP will then verify that the ISBN number you provided is registered as belonging to that publishing imprint.

For more information on publishing imprints, go back and have a look at the sub-heading, Publishing Imprint, under Step 4.

Publication Date

If your book has been published previously, enter its first publication date here. Otherwise, leave this field blank, and Amazon KDP will establish the publication date once that occurs.

Print Options

This is a very important part of the process, so think it through before you commit.

Unless you are familiar with how each option looks when the book is printed, it would be wise to see a physical Proof before you hit the Publish button (refer to Step 10 for more on this).

Your choices here will not only impact the look and feel of your printed paperback, but they will also affect the Printing Cost, which in turn will impact on what Price you will need to set to cover the Printing Cost and still allow you to earn a reasonable Royalty on each sale.

Obviously, the lower the Printing Cost, the better, as long as you can still get the quality you want in the finished product. Once you have your manuscript and cover loaded, you can play around with these options and see what impact they have on the Printing Cost.

The other consideration here is what is 'normal', or what are customers' expectations for publications in your genre. If you vary too far from what is normally done with publications in your genre, you run the risk of standing out for all the wrong reasons, perhaps undoing all the good work you have put into presenting your book as a professionally produced paperback.

Interior and Paper Type

For print colour, you have a choice between colour or a black and white Interior. Most authors avoid colour unless it is absolutely essential. Colour print (e.g. for colour photographs, charts, diagrams, text, etc.) will push the Printing Cost of your book up significantly. As a result, the price you charge will have to rise to cover those costs and still allow for any profit you wish to make per sale. Unless you absolutely must have some items printed in colour, black and white will keep your print costs down and enable you to either set a lower price, or earn a healthy profit, or both.

Paper type is a choice between cream or white. Rather than choose what seems a good idea, have a look at other books in your genre. Choosing white paper for a novel, for example, can send a clear signal that your publication is self-published. As a general rule, white paper is used for textbooks and many non-fiction publications, or any publication where there are colour images, as white paper allows for higher contrast with the colour of the image, chart or diagram. Most novels are printed on cream paper.

As with so many other decisions, ultimately, the choice is yours to make.

Trim Size

This is where you set you Trim Size or book size. For more about the choices here, go back to the sub-heading, Book Size (Trim Size), under Step 3.

Bleed Settings

The choices here are 'Bleed' or 'No Bleed'. Generally, you will set this to 'No Bleed'.

Bleed allows for some overrun of images or other elements which will be printed right up to the edge of any of the pages. Bleed will ensure that the image extends just beyond the edge of the page so that when the page is trimmed after printing, there is no chance of a thin white line appearing between the printed image or element and the edge of the page.

If you still find this confusing, click on the option, 'What are bleed settings?', in this field, and then click on 'More about bleed'.

A novel, other story, or text with no images will not need any Bleed. Even if images are included (I included some maps in my fantasy novel, *As Fire is to Gold: The Complete Chronicles of the Ilaroi*) you will still opt for 'No Bleed' unless the maps will be printed up against one or more of the edges of a page.

Paperback cover finish

The choices here are Matte or Glossy. Have a look at what the norm is for books in your genre. I like glossy, even though many say that the norm for novels is matte. There really is no substitute for choosing one and then seeing what it looks and feels like when you get your Proof Copy (more about this in Step 10) before finalising the publishing process.

Manuscript

I would recommend waiting until you have read my advice in Step 7 before uploading your manuscript. There are a number of things you need to check before you are ready to do this.

This is where you upload your finalised manuscript file once all formatting and preparations for publication of the contents are complete. It is a simple matter, once your manuscript is in one of the formats that will be accepted by Amazon KDP (PDF, DOC, DOCX, HTML or RTF), of pressing the 'Upload paperback manuscript' button and then finding and uploading the relevant file.

The uploading process can take several minutes, depending on the size and complexity of your manuscript file. Plenty of time to make a cup of coffee or take a short break.

Once your manuscript file is accepted by Amazon KDP, you will be able to preview how it will appear to a reader using Book Preview at the bottom of the page. This option will not become available until both your cover and manuscript files have been accepted and reviewed.

Book Cover

Once again, I would recommend waiting until you have read my advice in Step 8 before uploading your cover. There are a number of things you need to check before you are ready to do this.

This is where you upload your finalised cover file once all formatting and preparations for publication of the contents are complete. It is a simple matter, once your cover is formatted as a 'Print-Ready' PDF, of pressing the 'Upload your cover' button and then finding and uploading the relevant file.

The uploading process can take several minutes, depending on the size and complexity of your cover file. Plenty of time to make another cup of coffee or take a short break.

Amazon KDP does offer the alternative of using their Cover Creator process to make your own book cover. While this is fine and is an option I am sure some authors use and are happy with, my view is that you will find better DIY cover creator processes elsewhere than the one offered here by Amazon. Go back and have a look at some of the options under Step 4 for more information about these.

Once your cover file is accepted by Amazon KDP, you will be able to preview how it will appear to a reader using Book Preview at the bottom of the page. This option will not become available until both your cover and manuscript files have been accepted and reviewed.

Book Preview

Once your manuscript and cover have been successfully uploaded, the 'Launch Previewer' button will become operable. This Print Previewer allows you to see how the front and back covers as well as the spine fit, or whether they are misaligned for any reason.

As it provides a 'two-page view', it also enables you to page through and see what each spread of pages looks like, all the way through to the end of the book.

Read all of the information in the sidebar to the left carefully. While the fit of the cover can only be checked with this viewer, an option at the top right of the Print Previewer screen allows you to download a PDF proof of the interior, which is actually much easier to work with than checking the contents through the viewer.

Once you are happy with the way the cover is positioned, and all of the contents, you can approve the cover and book contents by clicking on the 'Approve' button at the bottom right of the Print Previewer screen.

This approval is not locked in place until you publish your paperback. Regardless of whether you have clicked Approve here, you can still go back and upload an amended cover or manuscript and then go through the approval process again.

As noted above, at any stage while inputting the above information, you can press the 'Save as Draft' button at the bottom of the page, then exit and return later. Similarly, you can 'Save and Continue', yet still make changes right up until you decide you are ready to publish.

You will not be committed until you press the 'Publish Your Paperback Book' button on the third page, Paperback Rights and Pricing.

The Paperback Rights & Pricing Page

At any stage while inputting the following information, you can press the 'Save as Draft' button at the bottom of the page, then exit and return later. You will not be committed until you press the 'Publish Your Paperback Book' button at the bottom of this page.

Territories

Select the Territories for which you hold distribution rights. In most cases, authors will hold worldwide rights. If for some reason, that is not the case, identify the individual countries where you do hold the rights.

Pricing & Royalty

This is where you determine what profit, if any, you will make. Choose carefully and play around with various pricing options until you are satisfied. You can still make adjustments to your pricing after your book is published, but you don't want to confuse or annoy your customers unnecessarily.

List Price

Usually, an author sets a List Price (that is, the price at which Amazon will sell your book, noting that in some countries, some form of VAT or other tax may still be added to that price) for the US market (Amazon.com). They then let Amazon KDP derive the price for their six other marketplaces from that figure. Before doing that, you will need to decide whether you will opt for:

- the standard distribution deal, which will give you a Royalty of 60% (this is not 60% of the List Price; deduct the Printing Cost from the List Price, then calculate 60% of that figure), or
- The expanded distribution deal, which will give you a Royalty of 40%.

When you insert a price in the List Price field, Amazon KDP calculates the final Royalty payable to you by doing the calculation as outlined in the first dot point above. This enables you to play around with the List Price until you are happy with the outcome.

Consider comparable costs for books in your genre before settling on a final figure. While a high final Royalty may seem attractive, setting a List Price which many customers find unpalatable will inevitably impact on sales. Customers will often compare the price of your book with its competitors.

There are, of course, a number of ways to offer special deals and to vary your List Price as part of specific marketing strategies from time to time post-publication. See Chapter 9 for more about some of the commonly used marketing strategies.

Once you have settled on a price for the US market, click on '6 other marketplaces' to see how that translates to prices for those countries. You can then vary the prices for any of those markets to make them appear more sensible. You might, for example, change a price for the Australian market from a derived figure of A$21.86 to A$21.99.

Expanded Distribution

Expanded Distribution gives you better access to sales to bookstores, other online retailers, libraries and academic institutions. While this might seem like a good thing, many of those don't like working with Amazon. An alternative favoured by many authors (myself included) is to also publish with IngramSpark as soon as you have published with Amazon.

While IngramSpark cannot compete with Amazon's overall place in the marketplace (it is estimated that some 70% of online sales of books currently go through Amazon), they do offer a better deal to bookstores, libraries and the like and are therefore favoured by them. This makes them a useful *addition* to your Amazon option.

Publishing through IngramSpark is relatively easy, though nowhere near as slick or simple as publishing through Amazon. You can use the same files that you used for your Amazon publication — **as long as you didn't opt for Amazon's free ISBN, which can only be used with Amazon, or for their Expanded Distribution network, both of which will force you to have a different ISBN for IngramSpark.**

It also attracts a small upfront fee (currently US$49 to publish both a paperback and an eBook, or just a paperback). IngramSpark also charges a fee for any amendments to your cover or manuscript files post-publication, something which Amazon KDP does not do.

One further benefit of publishing through IngramSpark is that they will publish a hardback edition. This is treated as another publication, needs its own unique ISBN, and attracts a further US$49 fee. The cover file for your paperback will need some work before it can be used for a hardback.

There are two options for how a hardback is made, both requiring a slightly larger cover than the one you used for a paperback, even though it may have exactly the same trim size. An experienced cover designer should be able to vary your paperback cover to suit IngramSpark's hardcover requirements for a very low cost.

I always publish my paperbacks through Amazon and then through IngramSpark as well, regardless of whether I intend to opt for a hardback edition as well.

Terms & Conditions

Amazon explains that, after you have decided to proceed with publication, it can still take up to 72 hours for your book to become available on Amazon's online store(s). In many cases, it happens much quicker than this.

Request a printed proof prior to publishing

Step 10 outlines the importance of requesting a physical Proof copy of your book before publishing. Suffice to say at this point — this is a critical cautionary step to take. It will cost you the Printing Cost plus postage, and the time it takes for a Proof to be sent to you through the mail, but you don't want to publish and then find you have missed something in quality control. The result could be a number of disgruntled customers receiving books that are blemished or marred in some way.

Force yourself to be patient, wait for the Proof Copy to be mailed to you, check it, and then proceed.

Note that the Proof copy is marked so that it cannot then be sold. It will have the words NOT FOR RESALE stamped across the cover.

Publish Your Paperback Book

Once you are sure everything is right, and you have slept on the decision to make sure you haven't forgotten anything, you are ready to 'Publish Your Paperback Book'.

Creating an eBook Entry on the Bookshelf

You create an entry for your eBook by clicking on the plus sign for a Kindle eBook under Create a New Title. Once you do this, you will immediately be taken to a page with three tabs, or sub-pages. The first is the Kindle eBook Details Page. The second is the Kindle eBook Content Page, and the third is the Kindle eBook Pricing Page. All three must be completed before you are ready to publish your eBook.

The Kindle eBook Details Page

At any stage while inputting the following information, you can press the 'Save as Draft' button at the bottom of the page, then exit and return later. Similarly, you can 'Save and Continue', yet still make changes right up until you decide you are ready to publish.

You will not be committed until you press the 'Publish Your Kindle eBook' button on the third sub-page, Kindle eBook Pricing.

Language

Select the primary language your book is written in from the dropdown menu.

Book Title

This is a very important field, for a number of reasons, the primary one being that **once your eBook is published, the title cannot be changed**, it is set in stone. You can change it as often as you like before you decide to publish your eBook, but not after that step has been taken.

Amazon also advises that books are linked automatically if the author name and book title of both formats (eBook and paperback) match exactly. They say that during the publishing process, KDP tries to match book details like title and author name to other editions available in the Amazon catalogue. Linking these formats provides the ideal browsing experience for their customers, so they advise you to make sure the title and author name you entered for your eBook and paperback match exactly.

This is advice that you should follow. Having your eBook and your paperback or other editions linked is a good thing from a marketing point of view. It is hard to see how having different titles for what is essentially the same book can work to your advantage. It would, however, confuse your readers no end.

The Subtitle field is optional.

Series

If your book is part of a series, you can put the series name here. This can be useful. I first published my novel in two parts: *As Fire is to Gold*, which was Book 1 of the Chronicles of the Ilaroi, and *When All the Leaves Have Fallen*, which was Book 2 of the Chronicles of the Ilaroi.

I used the Series field to indicate the name of the series — *Chronicles of the Ilaroi*. For Book 1, As *Fire is to Gold*, I entered the number '1' in the Series Number field. *When All the Leaves Have Fallen* was, of course, number '2'.

One of the advantages of this was that, once both books had been published, I was able to ask Amazon to create a Series Page on their website.

As a side note, I later combined these two books into one volume by creating a third publication. As I liked the title of Book 1, but a new publication had to have a different name, I titled it, *As Fire is to Gold: The Complete Chronicles of the Ilaroi*. This was not an ideal solution. It would have been better if I had thought this through before I published the first two books. You learn from your experiences.

The image on the next page shows you what my Series Page looks like on Amazon's website.

Edition Number

This field is relevant if you are publishing a book which you can expect might have subsequent further editions. I expect to update the book you are reading, for example, as aspects of the self-publishing process change or improve over time. Knowing this, I have put the number '1' in the Edition Number field.

Author

> Warning: This field may seem fairly innocuous, but you should treat it
> carefully.

Once the publishing process is complete, the way you have input your author
name here will be the way it is for this book forevermore. If I put 'Mr Mark
McCabe', for example, then that would be my author name on the Amazon
or any other distributor's sales page. Similarly, if I put 'Mark A. McCabe', that
would be the name that would appear. Just as with your book title, whatever
option you choose for **your author name in this field cannot be changed
after publication**.

If you subsequently decide you prefer just plain 'Mark McCabe', then any books subsequently published under that name will appear separately to those published by 'Mark A. McCabe' or 'Mr Mark McCabe'. Think this through carefully before you make your choice.

Your choice of how you display your author name can work to your advantage if you want it to. Joanna Penn, a well-known author and blogger, publishes non-fiction books as 'Joanna Penn' and supernatural thrillers as 'J.F.Penn'. As she says, she is not trying to hide her identity by having two different names for publication, she simply has different audiences and therefore different profiles and different marketing for the two categories of work she produces.

In a similar vein, there is nothing to stop you from publishing under a 'pen name'. Your Amazon account will be under your real name, but your book will be linked to your author or 'pen' name. You will need to take a few additional steps when setting up your Amazon Author Page so that it is properly linked to your account, but this is not difficult. I will walk you through how to do that in Chapter 7.

Contributors

This is where you can add any other people involved in the creation of your book other than yourself as the author. Amazon KDP advises that this could include editors, illustrators, translators, and anyone else you want to give credit to, as long as they worked on the book. You can enter multiple contributors.

It is your choice whether you add other contributors. I suspect that most authors only add those who have contributed content, such as illustrators and the like.

Make sure that if you are going to add other persons, you have checked that they are happy for you to do so. It wouldn't hurt for them to put that in writing (an email is considered to be 'in writing').

Description

This is another very important field. The contents of this field will appear on your Amazon sales page. If a potential customer looking for a book to buy online likes the look of your cover, this description is invariably what they will look at next to help them make their decision whether to buy it or not.

You need to put some time and effort into getting this just right. Just as for the blurb on your cover, do some Googling and have a look at some of the advice on the internet about how to write a good description. Perhaps start with this page — https://blog.reedsy.com/book-description/ — and then see what else you can find. Don't forget there is a text limit of 3,988 characters for your description, so don't write War and Peace!

You can change the contents of this field after your book is published, and you will probably find yourself doing just that, tinkering with it and fine-tuning it, or simply refreshing it with a new look every so often. You do, however, still want a good description on your sales page when your book is first published.

When I am first creating my book entry on my Bookshelf, I tend to simply put 'Expand later' here, and then work on my description offline until I am ready to complete this field properly.

One bugbear is that you cannot format the text here. Although you will be able to directly replace it, along with a little bit of formatting, through your Amazon Author Page after publication (more about this in Chapter 7), every time you update this page on your Bookshelf subsequent to publication, the contents of this field will overwrite anything you have entered through the Amazon Author Page.

Kindlepreneur.com provide an excellent free online book description generator tool which will format your book description for you. You still have to come up with the content, but it takes your description, along with your choice of formatting, and generates a coded version which you can then copy and paste into the Description field so that it displays on Amazon's Sales Page exactly how you intended it to. I have bookmarked this internet page in my browser and use it regularly.

Publishing Rights

If you wrote your manuscript, you own the copyright and hold the necessary publishing rights. If that is the case, you will click on the first radio button in this field. Click on the links provided in this field if you are in any doubt.

Keywords

This is yet another important field. It is optional, but overlook it at your peril. Put simply, Keywords are words that Amazon's behind-the-scenes software look for when a potential buyer is searching for a book. Amazon uses any keywords that appear in their search text to direct them to a page or pages (i.e. to books) that match their declared interest. Getting your keywords right, then, is of critical importance in drawing potential customers to your book page.

Once again, the best way to tackle this is to do a bit of research on the internet. Amazon KDP offers some help in this regard. Go to KDP's Help Topics and do a search for 'Choose Browse Categories'. Once you find that page, scroll down until you reach the sub-heading, 'Categories with keyword requirements'. Click on your genre, and you will find a useful list of keywords to get you started.

Don't stop there, however. There is an immense amount of useful information out there to help you. Do a Google search for keywords relevant to your specific genre.

As you can add to or amend this field subsequent to publication, one useful approach after your book has been published is to run a simple advertisement for a very small expenditure (perhaps $20 to $30, or even less) through Amazon to test a number of keywords and see which are the most successful in drawing buyers to your book page. You will find more about this in Chapter 9.

Using a good keyword, or keywords, won't guarantee sales, but it can ensure potential customers at least find your book. Whether they then buy it is going to depend on all those other issues we have already discussed — the cover, the blurb, the description, etc. None of these factors can come into play, however, until you can get a potential buyer to your book page.

Amazon KDP allow you to use up to seven keywords.

Categories

Categories, fortunately, are much simpler to identify then Keywords. Simply click on the 'Set categories' button and follow the most likely path for your book, given its content and genre. Think of it as being similar to the categories a physical bookstore uses to separate different types of books. Most bookstores will have a Crime / Mystery section, a Sci-Fi and Fantasy section, perhaps a Romance section, a Travel section, and so on. Categories work in the same way though they drill down further within those very broad categories.

Amazon KDP allow you to choose up to two categories.

Age and Grade Range

This field enables you to set a Children's book age range and a US grade age range. Both are optional.

Pre-Order

This enables you to make your eBook available for pre-order, for a period of up to 90 days before your publication date. This can be a useful feature which is not available for your paperback. It allows you to do some marketing of your book to build up expectations prior to it becoming available. The alternative to enabling pre-orders is to publish as soon as you have everything ready, which could then make your eBook available for sale within a matter of a few hours after you press the final button.

If you do decide to go down the pre-order path, consider what you will do with the publication of your paperback if you intend to have one as well as the eBook.

Selecting 'I am ready to release my book now' in this field will not send your eBook to publication. You will still need to input all of the information required on the remaining screens and publication will not occur until you press the 'Publish Your Kindle eBook' button on the third sub-page, Kindle eBook Pricing.

As noted above, at any stage while inputting the above information, you can press the 'Save as Draft' button at the bottom of the page, then exit and return later. Similarly, you can 'Save and Continue', yet still make changes right up until you decide you are ready to publish.

You will not be committed until you press the 'Publish Your Kindle eBook' button on the third sub-page, Kindle eBook Pricing.

The Kindle eBook Content Page

Once again, at any stage while inputting the following information, you can press the 'Save as Draft' button at the bottom of the page, then exit and return later. Similarly, you can 'Save and Continue', yet still make changes right up until you decide you are ready to publish.

You will not be committed until you press the 'Publish Your Kindle eBook' button on the third sub-page, Kindle eBook Pricing.

Manuscript

I would recommend waiting until you have read my advice in Step 7 before uploading your eBook manuscript. The format required is different from that for a paperback, and there are a number of things you need to check before you are ready to do this.

Digital Rights Management

This is an important setting, as it cannot be changed after your eBook has been published. Essentially, it is about whether you will allow a reader or buyer to share your work with others. While some authors do not want this to happen, others see it as a useful way of promoting their work to a wider audience.

Have a close look at the advice Amazon KDP provide about how this works before making your choice.

Upload Manuscript

This is where you upload your finalised manuscript file once all formatting and preparations for publication of the contents are complete. Be aware that the format required for an eBook is different from that required for a print edition, both in terms of the required layout and in the types of files that will be accepted. **This will be discussed in further detail in Step 7. I suggest that you hold off uploading your eBook manuscript until that point**.

It is a simple matter, once your manuscript has been set out in the appropriate manner and is in one of the formats that will be accepted by Amazon KDP (.doc, .docx, HTML, MOBI, EPUB, RTF, Plain Text and KPF are the primary formats), of pressing the 'Upload eBook manuscript' button and then finding and uploading the relevant file.

The uploading process can take several minutes, depending on the size and complexity of your manuscript file. Plenty of time to make a cup of coffee or take a short break.

Once your manuscript file is accepted by Amazon KDP, you will be able to preview how it will appear to a reader using eBook Preview at the bottom of the page. This option will not become available until both your cover and manuscript files have been accepted and reviewed.

Kindle eBook Cover

Once again, I would recommend waiting until you have read my advice in Step 8 before uploading your eBook cover. There are a number of things you need to check before you are ready to do this.

This is where you upload your finalised cover file once all formatting and preparations for publication of the contents are complete. It is a simple matter, once your cover is formatted as a JPG or TIFF file, of pressing the 'Upload your cover' button and then finding and uploading the relevant file.

The uploading process can take several minutes, depending on the size and complexity of your cover file. Plenty of time to make another cup of coffee or take a short break.

Amazon KDP does offer the alternative of using their Cover Creator process to make your own book cover. While this is fine and is an option I am sure some authors use and are happy with, my view is that you will find better DIY cover creator processes elsewhere than the one offered here by Amazon. Go back and have a look at some of the options under Step 4 for more information about these.

Once your cover file is accepted by Amazon KDP, you will be able to preview how it will appear to a reader using their Kindle eBook Previewer at the bottom of the page. This option will not become available until both your cover and manuscript files have been accepted and reviewed.

Kindle eBook Preview

Once your manuscript and cover have been successfully uploaded, the 'Launch Previewer' button will become operable. This Kindle eBook Previewer allows you to see the front cover as well as the contents of your eBook.

Read all of the information in the sidebar to the left carefully. While the fit of the cover can only be checked with this viewer, an option at the top right of the Print Previewer screen allows you to download a PDF proof of the interior, which is actually much easier to work with than checking the contents through the viewer.

Once you are happy with the cover and all of the contents, you can approve them by clicking on the 'Approve' button at the bottom right of the Kindle eBook Previewer screen. This approval is not locked in place until you publish your eBook. Regardless of whether you have clicked Approve here, you can still go back and add an amended cover or manuscript and then go through the approval process again.

As noted above, at any stage while inputting the above information, you can press the 'Save as Draft' button at the bottom of the page, then exit and return later. Similarly, you can 'Save and Continue', yet still make changes right up until you decide you are ready to publish.

You will not be committed until you press the 'Publish Your Kindle eBook' button on the third sub-page, Kindle eBook Pricing.

Kindle eBook ISBN

Unlike paperback publications, Amazon eBooks do not have to have an ISBN. Amazon assigns an ASIN instead, at no cost to you.

You may still wish to use an ISBN as well. Some of the other publishers you may decide to use subsequent to publishing your eBook through Amazon will require an ISBN, though most of them offer to provide you with one free of charge. You can read more about this in Chapter 6.

Step 5 covers the requirements associated with ISBNs in more detail. Go back and read those if you haven't already done so. My personal choice is that I use an ISBN for all of my publications, including eBooks through Amazon KDP. The choice is yours.

The reason I use my own ISBN is that I want to be absolutely sure that I retain all the rights to my book. If you do decide to use your own ISBN, and if you acquired that ISBN under the name of your own, or some other, publishing imprint, you must enter the name of that publishing imprint in the space provided for 'Publisher'. Amazon KDP will then verify that the ISBN number you provided is registered as belonging to that publishing imprint.

For more information on publishing imprints, go back and have a look at the sub-heading, Publishing Imprint, under Step 4.

The Kindle eBook Pricing Page

At any stage while inputting the following information, you can press the 'Save as Draft' button at the bottom of the page, then exit and return later. You will not be committed until you press the 'Publish Your Kindle eBook' button on the third sub-page, Kindle eBook Pricing.

KDP Select Enrolment

There are many articles on the internet about the pros and cons of enrolling in KDP Select, and I encourage you to have a look at some of them.

My analysis of the bulk of those articles is that the most popular choice is for an author to enrol their eBook in KDP Select for the first three months after publication, then to let that enrolment lapse and distribute through Smashwords and Draft2Digital in addition to Amazon KDP. The logic behind this is as follows:

- Enrolling in KDP Select opens up a number of marketing opportunities for your book. One of these is the option to offer your book either free or at a reduced price for a period up to five days. During this time, if it is promoted appropriately, as the number of downloads increases, it should climb up the Amazon rating list. Once the free or reduced-price period ends, for a short period at least, your book will benefit from its higher rating, increasing your likelihood of it being discovered by potential buyers.

- Enrolling your eBook in KDP Select means that it becomes exclusive to Amazon KDP for at least three months, at which point you can end the KDP Select Enrolment or continue for a further period.

- This means that you cannot distribute your book through channels other than those partnering with Amazon during your enrolment with KDP Select.

- Services such as Smashwords and Draft2Digital, while they do not have distribution channels that are anywhere near as effective as Amazon's, enable you to broaden the reach of your book by accessing some off the distributors that Amazon don't.

- You cannot, however, use Smashwords or Draft2Digital while you are enrolled in KDP Select.

The underlying premise to the logic above is that achieving a large number of downloads during its brief 'free' period on KDP Select will push your book high enough up Amazon's rating list for this to pay-off once that period ends. This depends, at least to some extent, on how effectively the 'free' period is promoted by you. There is no guarantee that this will succeed.

My suggestion is that you do some research on the internet and draw your own conclusions. One thing worth considering is that you can opt out of KDP Select after the three months is up. You are not locked in for a long period unless you choose to do so.

Territories

Select the Territories for which you hold distribution rights. In most cases, authors will hold worldwide rights. If, for some reason, that is not the case, identify the individual countries where you do hold the rights.

Royalty & Pricing

This is where you determine what profit, if any, you will make. Choose carefully and play around with various pricing options until you are satisfied. You can still make adjustments to your pricing after your book is published, but you don't want to confuse or annoy your readers unnecessarily.

70% or 35%

To get a 70% royalty, you must meet a certain number of conditions:

- You must price your eBook between US$2.99 and US$9.99.
- You will pay a small fee for file delivery to the customer.
- You won't get 70% in all territories, but you will get it in the US and most of Europe.
- Your eBook must not be in the public domain.
- Your eBook must be part of KDP Select if you want the 70% royalty in Brazil, India, Japan or Mexico.
- You must agree to allow buyers to lend their copy of your eBook to friends and family for up to 14 days.

Personally, I can't see a good reason not to opt for 70%. I don't enrol in KDP Select after the first three months, however. I am not concerned that this means I won't get 70% in Brazil, India, Japan or Mexico.

List Price

Usually, an author sets a List Price (that is, the price at which Amazon will sell your book, noting that in some countries, some form of VAT or other tax may still be added to that price) for the US market (Amazon.com). They then let Amazon KDP derive the price for their 12 other eBook marketplaces from that figure.

Once you insert a price in the List Price field, Amazon KDP calculates the royalty payable to you depending on which of the two royalty plans you have chosen. This enables you to play around with the List Price until you are happy with the outcome.

A recently added function, Kindle Pricing Support (Beta), lets you see the relationship between the price and past sales and author earnings for KDP books like yours. Selecting this option takes you to a page which displays a graph of the comparisons and suggests a List Price for your book which, based on historic data for KDP books similar to yours, would maximise your author earnings. It remains your choice whether to follow this advice or set a different price.

Regardless of whether you utilise the KDP Pricing Support advice, you should do some research of your own and consider comparable costs for books in your genre before settling on a final figure. While a high final royalty may seem attractive, setting a List Price which many customers find unpalatable will inevitably impact on sales.

There are, of course, a number of ways to offer special deals and to vary your List Price as part of specific marketing strategies from time to time post-publication. See Chapter 9 for more about some of the commonly used marketing strategies.

Once you have settled on a price for the US market, click on 'Other Marketplaces' to see how that translates to prices for those markets. You can then vary the prices for any of those markets to make them appear more sensible.

Matchbook

Kindle MatchBook gives customers who buy your paperback edition from Amazon.com the option to also purchase the eBook edition for $2.99 or less. If you have a paperback edition of your title on Amazon.com, you can enrol the eBook edition in Kindle MatchBook and earn royalties based on the Promotional List Price (choose from $2.99, $1.99, $0.99, or free) for any MatchBook sale.

Book Lending

If you agree to allow Book Lending, anyone who purchases your eBook can lend it to their friends and family for up to 14 days. If you opted for the 70% royalty plan, this would automatically be set to indicate you have agreed to Book Lending.

Terms & Conditions

Amazon explains that, after you have decided to proceed with publication, it can still take up to 72 hours for your book to become available on Amazon's online store(s). In many cases, it happens much quicker than this.

Publish Your Kindle eBook

Once you are sure everything is right, and you have slept on the decision to make sure you haven't forgotten anything, you are ready to 'Publish Your Kindle eBook'.

STEP 7 — CHECKLIST FOR FINALISING THE MANUSCRIPT

The following is a checklist for finalising your manuscript before you upload it to Amazon KDP, or to any other print-on-demand publisher for that matter. Most of the items listed below have already been discussed elsewhere but are repeated here so you can ensure your manuscript is ready to be uploaded.

Printed Publications (Paperback)

How to Format

There are several programs, applications or other paths you can choose to format your manuscript so that it is ready to be uploaded to your print publisher (in this case, Amazon KDP). These include, but are not limited to:

- Microsoft Word
- Google Docs
- Scrivener
- Vellum
- InDesign
- Reedsy.com

- engage an expert (many cover designers also offer manuscript layout services).

Trim Size (Book Size)

Choose the Trim Size you want to use for your publication. This impacts on many of the formatting issues. Refer to Step 3 for more detail on Trim Size.

Front Matter

The 'Front Matter' for your publication includes everything that comes before the first chapter. While there is no hard rule as to the sequence of in which items must be placed in the Front Matter (other than that the very first page should be the Title Page), there are some strong conventions. These include positioning the Copyright Page on the back of the first Facing Page (the Title Page), and that all other Front Matter pages are generally placed on Facing Pages.

While you can vary from these conventions, doing so may send a clear signal that your publication has been self-published. Have a look at the content and sequence of the Front Matter for books that have been published in your genre by some of the bigger publishing houses as a guide and then decide how you want it done in your book.

- *Page Breaks* — use a Page Break at the end of every section in the Front Matter (i.e., between different types of Front Matter pages). Do not use lines of space to achieve page breaks.
- *Title Page* — this should be the first page in your manuscript, which Amazon KDP will then consider the first Facing Page. Usually contains the book's title, the author's name, and may include the name of any Publishing Imprint.
- *Copyright Page* — usually positioned on the back of the Title Page. Should include the ISBN; may include the publishing imprint name and website, the author's website, any cover designer's name and website.
- *Hyperlinks* — remove all hyperlinks from any text anywhere in your print manuscript.

- *Dedications Page* — optional. Place on a Facing Page.
- *Acknowledgements Page* — optional. Place on a Facing Page.
- *Table of Contents* — optional. Start on a Facing Page.
- *List of Illustrations* — optional. Place on a Facing Page.
- *Maps or Charts* — optional. Start on a Facing Page.
- *Headers and Footers* — there should be no headers and footers on Front Matter Pages, with the possible exception of multiple pages bearing maps, illustrations and the like. These may be numbered using roman numerals, or some similar numbering.

Chapters

The chapters are where the primary content of your publication should be placed. Formatting issues to consider include:

- *Font and Font Size* — usually use a serif font for a print edition. The best font size is generally 11 or 12, unless the publication is a Large Print edition. All text in a Large Print edition (including Front and End Matter and Headers and Footers) should be at least font size 16, preferably 18, or higher.
- *Tabs* — The use of Tabs in your manuscript will most likely play havoc with any attempt to format your publication with consistency. Either do not use them or remove them before you do any serious formatting.
- Ensure *single spacing only between all sentences*.
- *Hyperlinks* — remove all hyperlinks from any text anywhere in your print manuscript.
- *Chapter Headings* — the first chapter should begin on a Facing Page. Normally the remaining chapters simply begin on the next page after the previous chapter finishes. Chapter headings should follow a consistent format throughout. They can be numbered or named. For novels, they are usually positioned part way down the page so that the chapter content always begins at the same position on the first page of each chapter.
- End all chapters with a Page Break.

- *Paragraph Format* — ensure consistent formatting for paragraphs within each chapter. Use Styles, if available, to ensure consistency.

- *First-Line Indents* — use a first-line indent for each paragraph within a chapter, except for the very first paragraph in each chapter, or the first paragraph after dot points or sub-headings, which should have no indent.

- *Justification* — ensure a consistent approach to justification for all paragraphs (except, of course, special paragraphs such as dot points, etc., which may have different justification to other text). For novels, the common approach to Justification is 'Justified' (that is, both left and right margins are even). Left Justification only is sometimes used as an alternative.

- *Alignment* — check that the top and bottom lines on each page align with the page beside it when the book is opened at any point.

- *Running Header* — use a Running Header for the Chapters. For novels, this normally has the Book Name on one page and the Author's Name on the next, and so on, throughout the book until the end of the last chapter. Non-fiction books may have the Book Name on one page and the Chapter Name, rather than Author Name, on the next. Ensure the Running Header applies to all chapters. Ensure there is no header on the first page of each chapter.

- *Page Numbers* — Place page numbers in the footers for the chapters only, beginning at '1' on the first page of the first chapter. Ensure page numbers continue sequentially with each new chapter and that they don't start again at 1.

End Matter

The 'End Matter' for your publication includes everything that comes after the final chapter. There is no hard rule as to the sequence in which items must be placed in the End Matter (or even if you should have any End Matter).

As with the Front Matter, any items you do include in End Matter should be separated by page breaks. Page numbering should end on the last page of the final chapter, and there should be no page numbers or headers on any of the End Matter pages. Information which could be included in End Matter includes, but is not limited to:

- a Glossary of Terms
- an Index
- an About the Author page
- a list or details of any Other Publications by the same author
- a Next Book Teaser.

File Format

For your print edition, Amazon KDP will accept a file containing the contents of your book (i.e. the final formatted manuscript with all of the pages and other required content) in the following formats:

- Microsoft Word (.doc or .docx)
- Adobe PDF (.pdf)
- Rich Text Format (.rtf).

Once both your cover and your manuscript are uploaded, assuming the files can be read by Amazon, you will be provided with access to an Online Previewer so you can visually check that the layout is as you require. If Amazon has any difficulties with the files you have uploaded, they will let you know what needs to be done to fix them.

DO NOT at this stage approve the uploaded content. You must check the content in the Online Previewer thoroughly before proceeding. Eyeball every single page (the pages are actually displayed two at a time, as in an open book, so that you can check that the two pages align with each other).

eBook Publications

How to Format

There are a number of programs, applications or other paths you can choose to format your manuscript so that it is ready to be uploaded to your print publisher (in this case, Amazon KDP). These include, but are not limited to:

- Kindle Create — for your Amazon KDP eBook, in particular, this is an excellent free tool provided by Amazon KDP. The file it creates, however, can only be used for your Amazon KDP eBook. It will not be recognised by other services such as Smashwords or Draft2Digital (see more about these in Chapter 6). It is easy to use and will strip out blank pages, remove headers and footers and perform a number of other tasks which you would need to do yourself otherwise. Kindle Create is free to download and use.
- Vellum
- Microsoft Word
- Google Docs
- Scrivener
- InDesign
- Reedsy.com
- Engage an expert (many cover designers also offer manuscript layout services). Be wary of taking this step, however, as formatting an eBook is usually far simpler than formatting a paperback. Many of the providers offering this service charge hundreds of dollars for something which can easily be completed in under an hour.

Trim Size (Book Size)

Choosing a Trim Size or Book Size is not necessary for your eBook. The page size for an eBook is determined by the application any given reader is using.

Front Matter

As for your print edition, the 'Front Matter' for your eBook includes everything that comes before the first chapter. While there is no hard rule as to the sequence of in which items must be placed in the Front Matter (other than that the very first page should be the Title Page), there are some strong conventions. These include positioning the Copyright Page immediately after the Title Page.

- *Page Breaks* — use a Page Break at the end of every page in the Front Matter. Do not use lines of space to achieve page breaks.
- *Blank Pages* — remove any blank pages from your eBook manuscript. There is no such thing as a Facing Page in an eBook (every page is a Facing Page), and thus no need for any blank pages.
- *Title Page* — Usually contains the book's title, the author's name, and may include the name of any Publishing Imprint.
- *Copyright Page* — usually positioned after the Title Page. You should include the ISBN (if there is one) and you may also include the publishing imprint name and website, the author's website, any cover designer and/or illustrator's name and their website.
- *Hyperlinks* — as opposed to your print edition, hyperlinks will work in an eBook, and it is a good idea to include them wherever appropriate. If you have taken the hyperlinks out for your print edition, put them back in for your eBook.
- *Dedications Page* — optional.
- *Acknowledgements Page* — optional.
- *Table of Contents* — optional.
- *List of Illustrations* — optional.
- *Maps or Charts* — optional.
- *Headers and Footers* — there should be no headers and footers in your eBook.

Chapters

The chapters are where the primary content of your publication should be placed. Formatting issues to consider include:

- *Font and Font Size* — usually use a sans serif font for an eBook, though serif fonts are sometimes used. There is no need to choose a font size as this can be adjusted by the reader to suit their preference.
- *Tabs* — The use of Tabs in your manuscript will most likely play havoc with any attempt to format your publication with consistency. Either do not use them or remove them before you do any serious formatting.
- Ensure *single spacing only between all sentences.*

- *Chapter Headings* — Chapter headings should follow a consistent format throughout. They can be numbered or named. For novels, they are usually positioned part way down the page so that the chapter content always begins at the same position on the first page of each chapter.
- End all chapters with a Page Break.
- *Paragraph Format* — ensure consistent formatting for paragraphs within each chapter.
- *First-Line Indents* — use a first-line indent for each paragraph within a chapter, except for the very first paragraph in each chapter, which should have no indent.
- *Justification* — ensure a consistent approach to Justification for all paragraphs (except of course, special paragraphs such as dot points, etc.). For novels, the common approach to Justification is 'Justified' (that is, both left and right margins are even). Left Justification only is sometimes used as an alternative.
- *Headers and Footers* — there should be no headers and footers in your eBook. There is also no need to include any page numbering.

End Matter

The 'End Matter' for your eBook includes everything that comes after the final chapter. There is no hard rule as to the sequence in which items must be placed in the End Matter (or even if you should have any End Matter).

As with the Front Matter, any items you do include in End Matter should be separated by page breaks. Information which could be included in End Matter includes, but is not limited to:

- a *Call to* Action — this is usually placed immediately after the end of the last chapter and may include either a link to your website or a link that enables the reader to be added to the author's mailing list
- a Glossary of Terms
- an Index
- an About the Author page
- a list or details of any Other Publications by the same author
- a Next Book Teaser.

File Format

For your eBook, Amazon KDP will accept a file containing the contents of your book (i.e. the final formatted manuscript with all of the pages and other required content) in the following formats:

- Kindle Create (.kpf).
- Microsoft Word (.doc or .docx)
- Adobe PDF (.pdf)
- Rich Text Format (.rtf)
- HTML
- MOBI
- EPUB
- Plain Text (.txt).

Kindle Create

Kindle Create is probably one of the easiest tools to use to format your eBook manuscript. Although Vellum (which can only be used on a Mac) does a very similar job and is even better in many ways, Kindle Create is free, and Vellum is relatively expensive.

Even if your manuscript is in one of the other file formats, Kindle Create (which can be downloaded for free from Amazon KDP) will adapt the format with some input from you, enable you to review it in an eReader similar to that used by people who purchase the eBook, and will then create a file for uploading. Google 'Kindle Create' to find and download a free version of the program for use on either a Mac or a PC. The website also provides a step-by-step tutorial and answers to Frequently Asked Questions.

Once both your cover and your manuscript are uploaded, assuming the files can be read by Amazon, you will be provided with access to an Online Previewer so you can visually check that the layout is as you require. If Amazon has any difficulties with the files you have uploaded, they will let you know what needs to be done to fix them.

DO NOT at this stage approve the uploaded content. You must check the content in the Online Previewer thoroughly before proceeding. Eyeball every single page.

STEP 8 — CHECKLIST FOR FINALISING THE COVER

The following is a checklist for finalising your book's cover before you upload it to Amazon KDP, or for any other print-on-demand publisher for that matter. Most of the items listed below have already been discussed elsewhere but are repeated here so you can ensure your cover is ready to be uploaded.

Printed Publications (Paperback)

Trim Size (Book Size)

Choose the Trim Size you want to use for your publication. This impacts on the size, and therefore the design, of your cover. Refer to Step 3 for more detail on Trim Size.

Finalise the manuscript formatting

Before you can finalise your cover, you must finalise the formatting of the interior. One of the key pieces of information arising from the finalisation of the manuscript is the total number of pages your book requires.

Amazon KDP provides a free calculator. Have a look at the Help Topics on the Amazon KDP website and look for KDP Tools and Resources. You will find a link to a downloadable calculator which, once you indicate your choice of paper type, trim size and the total number of pages in your manuscript, will give you all the dimensions necessary to create your cover. You can then send this information to your cover designer.

The total number of pages in the manuscript determines the thickness of your book and thus, the width of the spine. **You can, and probably should, however, begin work on your cover without this measurement**. Doing that will save unnecessary delay at the end of your publishing project. Whoever is doing the cover design for you can alter the dimensions of the cover and make any necessary adjustments once that figure is known definitively.

Do not, however, finalise your cover until you know the exact number of final pages. If you do this, you may find yourself having to outlay additional funds for an amendment to the cover which could have been easily avoided. Cover designers understand that this will often be the last bit of information supplied.

ISBN

You must know the ISBN for your book before you upload your cover. Amazon needs this so they can include it in the barcode which they will place on the back cover (see more about the barcode below) over the cover artwork you upload. Refer to Step 5 for more information about ISBNs.

Barcode

All print publications require a barcode which identifies, amongst other things, the ISBN. Amazon will provide one for free and will place it on top of any final cover file that you upload. As their cover templates identify exactly where they will place the barcode, you should send this to your cover designer so they can allow for that placement and not, for example, place any blurb (see below) in that space.

You can opt to provide your own barcode, in which case the cover file you upload should already include the barcode positioned where you choose to have it placed. Personally, I can't see much point in doing this. Although most ISBN sellers/providers also provide corresponding barcodes, it is far simpler to let Amazon KDP do this for you. They do not charge for that service.

Publishing Imprint

The desirability of including a publishing imprint has been discussed in some detail in Step 4. If you are going to include your own publishing imprint (something I highly recommend), you will need to send any artwork for the imprint to your cover designer so they can include it on the spine of your cover, and on the back cover if you so desire. Your cover designer may offer a service which includes design of a publishing imprint.

Blurb

The 'blurb' which goes on the back cover plays an important role in marketing your paperback to potential buyers wherever your book is being sold from physical bookstores or other physical outlets. Its importance and some advice on how to craft a good one is provided in Step 4.

Your cover designer will need to know the contents of your blurb before they can finalise your cover. Keep it short. You don't have a lot of space to play with, particularly when you leave room for a barcode.

Strapline or Sub-title

You may also decide to include a brief 'strapline', sub-title or other short text on the front cover of your book, regardless of whether you specified one on the Paperback Details page on your Bookshelf. Have a look at the front cover of this publication and you will see what I mean. If you wish to do this, you will need to let your cover designer know.

File Format

For your print edition, Amazon KDP requires a cover file that is formatted as a Print-Ready PDF. Any decent cover designer will know to provide your cover file to you in this format, but check with them before you sign-up or outlay any expenditure, just to be sure. If you are working on your own cover design, Amazon KDP's Help Text includes a topic entitled 'Create a Paperback PDF File' which explains some simple ways to turn your work into the correct PDF format.

Once both your cover and your manuscript are uploaded, and the files have been analysed and accepted by Amazon, you will be provided with access to an Online Previewer so you can visually check that the layout is as you require. If Amazon has any difficulties with the files you have uploaded, they will let you know what needs to be done to fix them.

DO NOT at this stage approve the uploaded content. **You must check the content in the Online Previewer thoroughly before proceeding**. Eyeball every single page (the pages are displayed two at a time, as in an open book, so that you can check that they align with each other).

eBook Publications

If you already have a cover for your print edition, you should be able to easily crop the front cover into a separate file. Your eBook cover will then be completed (though the necessary file may need to be converted to a different format — a relatively simple task). In that case, skip all the other information below and go straight to File Format at the bottom of this Step.

Trim Size (Book Size)

Choose the Trim Size you want to use for your publication. This impacts on the size, and therefore the design, of your cover. Refer to Step 3 for more detail on Trim Size. If you are only publishing an eBook, there is no need to choose a Trim Size.

Spine and Back Cover

EBooks don't have a spine or a back cover. They only have a front cover. You could, however, if you so desired, crop the back cover artwork from your print edition cover and use it as the final page in your eBook manuscript. This is not usually done but can, nonetheless, look effective. If you do this, remember to block out or remove the barcode, as the information in that will relate to the print edition and not to your eBook.

Strapline or Sub-title

You may decide to include a brief 'strapline', sub-title or other short text on the front cover of your book, regardless of whether you specified one on the eBook Details page on your bookshelf. Have a look at the front cover of this publication and you will see what I mean. If you wish to do this, you will need to let your cover designer know.

File Format

For your eBook publication, Amazon KDP requires a cover file that is formatted as a JPG or TIFF document (as opposed to the Print-Ready PDF format for your print edition). Any decent cover designer will know to provide your cover file to you in this format, but check with them before you sign-up or outlay any expenditure, just to be sure.

Once both your cover and your manuscript are uploaded, and the files have been analysed and accepted by Amazon, you will be provided with access to an Online Previewer so you can visually check that the layout is as you require. If Amazon has any difficulties with the files you have uploaded, they will let you know what needs to be done to fix them.

DO NOT at this stage approve the uploaded content. **You must check the content in the Online Previewer thoroughly before proceeding**. Eyeball every single page (the pages are actually displayed two at a time, as in an open book, so that you can check that the two pages align with each other).

STEP 9 — SETTING THE PRICE

Much of the following information has already been provided in Step 6. It is repeated here as this information should be reviewed as the penultimate step in the self-publishing process, followed only by ordering and checking a proof copy.

The price you wish to set for your publication can, of course, as stated elsewhere in this book, be amended at any time both before and after publication. It is best, however, to think through all of the pricing issues thoroughly before you put your publication up for sale, even if you do tinker with the List Price subsequently.

Printed Publications (Paperback)

Pricing & Royalty

The third sub-page of your Bookshelf entry, Paperback Rights & Pricing, is where you determine what profit, if any, you will make from your book. Choose carefully and play around with various pricing options until you are satisfied. You can still make adjustments to your pricing after your book is published, but you don't want to confuse or annoy your readers unnecessarily.

List Price

Usually, an author sets a List Price (that is, the price at which Amazon will sell your book, noting that in some countries, some form of VAT may still be added to that price) for the US market (Amazon.com) and then lets Amazon KDP derive the price for their six other marketplaces from that figure. Before doing that, you will need to decide whether you will opt for:

- the standard distribution deal, which will give you a Royalty of 60% (this is not 60% of the List Price; deduct the Printing Cost from the List Price, then calculate 60% of that figure), or
- The expanded distribution deal, which will give you a Royalty of 40%.

When you insert a price in the List Price field, Amazon KDP calculates the final royalty payable to you by doing the calculation as outlined above. This enables you to play around with the List Price until you are happy with the outcome.

Consider comparable costs for books in your genre before settling on a final figure. While a high final royalty may seem attractive, setting a List Price which many customers find unpalatable will inevitably impact on sales.

Once you have settled on a price for the US market, click on '6 other marketplaces' to see how that translates to prices for those countries. You can then vary the prices for any of those markets to make them appear more sensible. You might, for example, change a price for the Australian market from a derived figure of A$21.86 to A$21.99.

Expanded Distribution

Expanded Distribution gives you better access to sales to bookstores, other online retailers, libraries and academic institutions. While this might seem like a good thing, many of those don't like working with Amazon. An alternative favoured by many authors (myself included) is to also publish with IngramSpark as soon as you have published with Amazon.

While IngramSpark cannot compete with Amazon's place in the marketplace (it is estimated that some 70% of online sales of books currently go through Amazon), they do offer a better deal to bookstores, libraries and the like and are therefore favoured by them. This makes them a useful *addition* to your Amazon option.

Publishing through IngramSpark is relatively easy, though nowhere near as slick or simple as publishing through Amazon. You can use the same files that you used for your Amazon publication — **as long as you didn't opt for Amazon's free ISBN, which can only be used with Amazon, or for their Expanded Distribution network, both of which will force you to have a different ISBN for IngramSpark.**

It also attracts a small upfront fee (currently US$49 to publish both a paperback and an eBook, or just a paperback). IngramSpark also charges a fee for any amendments to your cover or manuscript files post-publication, something which Amazon KDP does not do.

One further benefit of publishing through IngramSpark is that they will publish a hardback edition. This is treated as another publication, needs its own unique ISBN, and attracts a further US$49 fee. The cover file for your paperback will need some work before it can also be used for a hardback. There are two options for how a hardback is made, both requiring a slightly larger cover than the one you used for a paperback even though it may have exactly the same trim size. An experienced cover designer should be able to vary your paperback cover to suit IngramSpark's hardcover requirements for a very low cost.

I always publish through Amazon and then through IngramSpark as well.

eBook Publications

Royalty & Pricing

The Kindle eBook Pricing Page on your bookshelf is where you determine what profit, if any, you will make from sales of your eBook. Choose carefully and play around with various pricing options until you are satisfied. You can still make adjustments to your pricing after your book is published, but you don't want to confuse or annoy your readers unnecessarily.

70% or 35%

To get a 70% royalty, you must meet a certain number of conditions. These include the following items.

- You must price your eBook between US$2.99 and US$9.99
- You will pay a small fee for file delivery to the customer
- You won't get 70% in all territories, but you will get it in the US and most of Europe
- Your eBook must not be in the public domain
- Your eBook must be part of KDP Select if you want the 70% royalty in Brazil, India, Japan or Mexico
- You must agree to allow buyers to lend their copy of your eBook to friends and family for up to 14 days.

I can't see a good reason not to opt for 70%. I don't enrol in KDP Select after the first three months, however. I am not concerned that this means I won't get 70% in Brazil, India, Japan or Mexico.

List Price

Usually, an author sets a List Price (that is, the price at which Amazon will sell your book, noting that in some countries, some form of VAT or other tax may still be added to that price) for the US market (Amazon.com). They then let Amazon KDP derive the price for their 12 other eBook marketplaces from that figure.

Once you insert a price in the List Price field, Amazon KDP calculates the royalty payable to you depending on which of the two royalty plans you have chosen. This enables you to play around with the List Price until you are happy with the outcome.

A recently added function, Kindle Pricing Support (Beta), let's you see the relationship between the price and past sales and author earnings for KDP books like yours. Selecting this option takes you to a page which displays a graph of the comparisons and suggests a List Price for your book which, based on historic data for KDP books similar to yours, would maximise your author earnings. It remains your choice whether to follow this advice or set a different price.

Regardless of whether you utilise the KDP Pricing Support advice, you should do some research of your own and consider comparable costs for books in your genre before settling on a final figure. While a high final royalty may seem attractive, setting a List Price which many customers find unpalatable will inevitably impact on sales.

Once you have settled on a price for the US market, click on 'Other Marketplaces' to see how that translates to prices for those markets. You can then vary the prices for any of those markets to make them appear more sensible.

STEP 10 — THE IMPORTANCE OF PROOF COPIES

Getting a Proof Copy is an absolutely essential cautionary step to take before deciding to proceed with publication. Skip this step at your peril!

In the case of one of my earliest self-publication efforts, I decided to do just that — to skip requesting a Proof Copy for my paperback publication. I had been through the self-publication process previously and knew all of the things I had to do to get it right. I had also checked the electronic proof quite thoroughly — or so I thought.

One of the considerations in requesting a physical Proof Copy is the cost. Although you only pay the Printing Cost for the copy, you must also pay for postage and delivery. In my case, as I was living in New Zealand at the time, the postage cost for one book was quite substantial (close to NZ$15.00). I also knew that the cover of a Proof Copy clearly identifies it as a Proof which is not for sale.

As I was keen to get the book onto the market, I decided to proceed to publication without first sighting a physical Proof Copy. I pressed the publication button and then proceeded to purchase one Author Copy for my own bookshelves. An Author Copy (see more about this in Chapter 5) is identical to the published version, only at a reduced price to the author, so they can purchase copies to use at book launches, book signings and other such events, or to sell directly to customers themselves.

To my horror, when the book arrived several days later and I opened it up to thumb through the pages, I found that text in the second half of the book was completely misaligned, causing it to be half off the page, leaving the bottom half of each page blank. This was my precious book which had been for sale on Amazon's online bookstore for more than a week already.

After an hour or so trying to find out what had gone wrong, I finally discovered that when I had converted my Microsoft Word document to a PDF format (something I didn't need to do, as Amazon KDP accept files in Microsoft Word format), a very slight difference in the margin setting for all of the paragraphs in the latter chapters had played havoc with the conversion, causing the misalignment I have described above. I quickly rectified the mistake and uploaded a corrected version for publication.

Fortunately, I had not done any marketing during that initial period and had thus made no sales. Had the opposite been the case, I could have been left with some very annoyed customers and my reputation as a self-publisher in tatters. The only bright side was that we learn from our mistakes. I will never publish a print edition in future without first requesting, and then thoroughly checking, a physical proof copy.

EBooks have electronic proof copies only. The same need for close checking of the proof, however, applies as does for a print edition. You must check your proofs carefully, eyeballing every page with an eye for any obvious errors. You shouldn't need to read through it again. That kind of checking should have already been done. What you are looking for in the proof copy is format and layout issues in particular.

If it is the physical Proof Copy of a print or paperback edition, check all of the text justification, make sure the appropriate pages are all on Facing Pages and keep a close eye on the Headers and Footers as well as the alignment of the top and bottom lines in all of the chapters. **Go through every single page. It won't take as long as you might think and it will be well worth the investment in time**.

I would recommend one additional step — purchase an Author Copy if it is a print edition or an eBook edition as soon as each becomes available for purchase. Satisfy yourself that what is on sale is exactly as it should be.

The type of error that I described above was nobody's fault but my own. It could have been easily avoided.

STEP 11 — PUBLISH

You are now ready to publish your book, be it as a printed publication (a paperback) or an eBook. But hold on! Bear with me and read the rest of what I have to say below before you push the button — or buttons.

So, you're ready to publish. What will happen then? Within a few hours, or perhaps a few days, both your paperback and your eBook will be available for sale on Amazon. Fantastic. What an achievement! But what else will happen then? How will anyone know your book is out there, other than your close friends and family, or anyone else you ring or email to share the happy news with? And once you're published, is that it? Do you just sit back and put your feet up now?

Of course you can do that — if just being published was your end goal. If you have longer-term goals as an author, however, you'll probably want to try to generate some sales or build a platform to build sales from if and when your portfolio of written work starts to grow even further.

With that in mind, the following are just a few of the issues you should have a 'heads-up' about before you press the 'publish button'. Most of these will be covered in more detail over the next few chapters. For the moment, however, just a few words about each. Then you can decide what you want to know more about, if anything.

A word of caution, however. This book is about how to publish, not about how to market or sell books, or how to build a profile as an author. Whole books and countless articles have been written about marketing alone, let alone any of the other subjects below. Consider some of the chapters that follow as providing introductory comments and advice on these matters — enough to get you started or to give you an idea of where to look for more information.

Author Copies

Once you're published through Amazon KDP, you will become eligible for Author Copies of your printed publication. You can purchase these at the Printing Cost plus postage and delivery. If you buy in bulk, say 10 to 20 copies at a time, you will probably find that the cost per copy is well under $10, perhaps down as low as $5 or $6, depending on the size of your book. This creates an ideal situation for you to sell copies of your book locally, at markets or fairs, after book readings, and so on.

Perhaps you will want to give some copies away after a Book Launch or sell them at a discounted price. It's up to you. You can find out more about Author Copies in the next chapter — Chapter 5.

Publishing with other providers

Once you are published through Amazon KDP, you may want to publish your print edition with IngramSpark as well to provide a more attractive deal for other online retailers, libraries or universities. Or you may want to take advantage of their option of creating a hardback edition.

With your eBook, Amazon has the 'lion's share' of the market. Publishing with Smashwords and Draft2Digital as well, however, will bring other benefits, at little or no additional cost. You can find out more about this in Chapter 6.

Marketing

Many authors say that the real work begins after you are published, regardless of whether you are traditionally published or self-published. Marketing is a whole new world altogether, with some things being quite easy to achieve and others requiring a great deal more effort. It is your choice as to how far you go with marketing. You can find out more about some of the options open to you for marketing your publications in Chapter 9.

Your Amazon Book Page and Author Pages

One of the easiest and quickest ways to begin marketing your publication(s) is to set up your Amazon Author Page and your Amazon Book Page(s). This can be done quite easily. If you do nothing, Amazon will create a Book Page for your publication(s), but it will be devoid of much of the information your customers are likely to be looking for. It is not hard to address this and doing so will be in your best interests. You can find out more about this in Chapter 7.

Sales Reports

Once you are published, you will begin to have access to a range of Sales Reports from Amazon KDP (IngramSpark and most of the other publishing companies provide similar information to their authors). It pays to know where to find these, what their limitations are, and how you can monitor sales on your book on a daily basis should you want to. Observing what is happening with your book on the sales front can provide a feedback loop that will help you fine-tune how you present it. You can find out more about this in Chapter 10.

Other Marketing

Under Step 6, I outlined the importance of Keywords. Once you are published these will become an important factor influencing how easy (or difficult) it will be for potential customers to find your book out of the hundreds of thousands if not millions for sale on the internet. Go back and read that advice before you publish.

Chapter 9 will provide you with more information, including a cost-effective way to fine-tune the keywords for your book by running some low-cost advertisements for a brief period.

Libraries

Getting your book into libraries can help spread the word. There are several ways of achieving this, apart from just visiting the libraries near you with your book in hand. You can find out more about this in Chapter 11.

'Legal Deposit' with your National Library

Many authors don't know that they are expected under their country's laws to place a copy of their published book with their National Library. Although this is not the case everywhere, a great many countries do have such requirements. You can find out more about this in Chapter 11 as well.

Delayed Publication Date

Amazon KDP allow you to take pre-orders (they do all of this for you through their online stores) for your eBook prior for up to 90 days before a scheduled publication date. This is not possible with your printed publication (paperback). See more about this issue in Chapter 5 — Author Copies.

Publish and Celebrate!

Finally, you are ready to publish your book. Press the appropriate button on the third sub-page of your Bookshelf for either your eBook or your paperback edition (or both) and sit back and wait for Amazon to do its final checks and load your book(s) onto their online store. Amazon advises that this can take up to 72 hours, but it often takes less time than this. They will send you a confirming email once your publications go 'Live'.

Start letting your friends, family and others know and get ready to crack open the champagne. Now's also the time to make sure any marketing strategies you have in mind are already up and running or are ready to go.

Congratulations. Do some cartwheels — even if they are only in your mind. You are now a published author!

STEP 12 — AMENDING OR UPDATING POST-PUBLICATION

Once your book is published, some of its elements are 'set in stone'. They cannot be amended. Most, however, including the contents and the cover, can be amended at any time of your choosing. As what Amazon KDP offers is a 'Print-on-Demand' service, supplies of your book never sit in boxes in a warehouse awaiting a purchase. The next order received by Amazon after any amendment you have made has been processed will simply be printed using the most recent approved update to your publication.

Elements such as the title of your book and the author name under which it has been processed, as well as the ISBN and the name of any Publishing Imprint which owns the ISBN, cannot be changed post-publication. All of the rest can be amended whenever you deem it necessary. Elements which are most commonly amended, sometimes on a regular basis, include:

- the book description
- the keywords
- the manuscript itself, most commonly in order to fix spelling or other similar mistakes, or to make changes to the layout
- the cover, either a wholesale change and a fresh approach, variations to the blurb, or inclusion of snippets from favourable reviews, etc.

No matter how good an editing process your book has gone through, it is inevitable that you will still find errors after it has been published. Don't beat yourself up about these, just get in and fix them. Once that is done, you can upload a new manuscript file and get it approved and accepted so that future orders are based on that rather than on the file which contained errors.

There is no restriction on how often you do such updates. Although it makes sense to wait a small period, especially in the early days after publication, when you are most likely to discover any errors that are still hiding away in your manuscript, there is nothing to stop you updating the file as often as you want to.

Implementing these and any other changes is a simple process. Go into the relevant fields on your Bookshelf and make amendments whenever and wherever you decide they are necessary. If you are making changes to the manuscript or the cover, make these changes in the necessary files and then upload them as replacements, going through the same process you have already gone through pre-publication to review and check the relevant proofs and approve what has been uploaded.

Regardless of what changes you make, or how many there are, your publication will only be updated (effectively, republished), after you press the 'Publish' button on the third sub-page of your Bookshelf entry. Until that time, as long as you press the Save button at the bottom of the screen on which you are making changes, the changes will sit there until you decide to republish.

As with the initial publishing process, once the 'Publish' button has been pressed, it may take several hours, or even a day or more in some cases, before the changes are accepted by Amazon KDP and become the basis for filling future orders. As with your initial publication, Amazon will send you a confirming email once your changes go 'Live'.

---

5. AUTHOR COPIES

Your book has been published or will be as soon as Amazon load it onto their online stores, and you want to order a copy (or copies) of the print edition for yourself. The good news is that you don't need to buy copies at full price through the Amazon store like everyone else — even though you would get your royalty back on those purchases eventually. As the author, you are entitled to purchase 'author copies'.

How to order Author Copies

Now that your book has been published, you will notice that the yellow button beside your book entry on the Bookshelf is now a light grey colour. The label 'Continue setup' has now been replaced by 'Enrol in KDP' for your eBook edition and by 'Promote and Advertise' for your paperback. Beside the buttons, you will notice smaller buttons labelled with three dots. If you press the button with the dots for your paperback, you will now see that one of the options is 'Order author copies'.

You can order any quantity from one up to 999. The more copies you buy at one time, the lower the overall cost will be because it is cheaper to ship copies in bulk than it is to ship them to you a few at a time.

Be careful, however! Don't be too ambitious. If you order 50 copies, and can't either sell or give them all away, you could end up being stuck with a cupboard full of books. That might also mean that you've spent some money you haven't been able to get a return on. Unless you have a very good idea not only of what you want to do with all those author copies but also of your chances of achieving whatever goal or goals you might have, it's better to start small until you have a good idea of likely demand.

You should also note that you will have to choose which marketplace you want to order your author copies from. Amazon KDP does not distribute author copies from all of their stores. As I currently live in New Zealand, for example, I have had to purchase my author copies from the amazon.com store. This is not a problem, though it can push your shipping and delivery costs up (see more about this under Cost of Author Copies below). In my case, I found the shipping cost from the US store quite reasonable when I was ordering bulk copies in the one order. Shipping just one copy at a time, however, proved to be prohibitive.

Cost of Author Copies

Amazon charges the Printing Cost, which is always shown at the bottom of sub-page two on your Bookshelf (once you have approved the manuscript content and cover which you uploaded), plus the cost of shipping and delivery. Because of the shipping and delivery charge, the more author copies you order at one time, the lower the unit cost will be.

Nonetheless, buying author copies opens up the prospect of you achieving a higher profit per book on those copies than you would on copies sold through Amazon's online store. For my first book, I purchased 20 author copies to start out. The unit cost, taking into account the Printing Cost and the shipping and delivery charges, came in at around $8.50. I subsequently sold many of these at $20.00 per copy, which still represented a saving to the purchasers, as they didn't have to pay for shipping costs from Amazon. Instead of a royalty of $5.26 per copy, my profit from the sale of author copies was $11.50 per copy.

Of course, this doesn't mean that I will try to sell all of my books myself rather than through Amazon. I wouldn't even try to compete with their reach and breadth of distribution networks. For a small volume of sales, however, I can make a nice profit by selling some of my books myself.

Many authors purchase a small number of their books in this way and then market them to customers directly from their author website (see more about this in Chapter 8). They charge a small fee for postage and delivery but offset some of this cost against their profits in order to stay competitive with someone considering buying direct from Amazon. Because of the size of their operations, Amazon will almost always have a lower postage and delivery fee than the author can achieve.

Uses of Author Copies

What might you do with a supply of author copies? The following are just some of the more obvious uses:

- Keep some copies for yourself, giving them pride of place on your own bookshelf.
- Give some away to friends and family. Don't forget, however, that many of your first customers will come from these groups.
- Ask local bookstores to put them on their shelves and sell them for you (more about this in Chapter 9). If you succeed in gaining their cooperation, they are likely to ask for only two or three copies to start with to see how they go.
- Have some on hand to give away in free promotions.
- Have some available to sell at literary or other events such as book readings, a book launch, fairs, fêtes, and so on.
- Sell some from your own website (see my comments on this under Cost of Author Copies above, and in Chapter 9).

6. THE BENEFITS OF USING COMPLEMENTARY PUBLISHERS

I have put the case several times in this publication for Amazon KDP being the provider of choice for authors wishing to self-publish. Their attributes include their low cost, their very reasonable royalty rates, the ease of working with them and their online interface, their extensive and easy-to-follow Help topics, their wide-range of useful tools and other resources and last, but not least, their extensive distribution network and their dominance of the online book retail market.

There are, nonetheless, some very good reasons for using a few of the other providers in this space to complement, or as an add-on to, what Amazon KDP provides. The providers mentioned below are not the only other providers in this space — there are many. From what I have observed, these tend to be the most popular ones. There are good reasons for that, as I will outline below.

I use all of the following three. I publish my paperback and my eBook on Amazon KDP first, and then I proceed to publish my paperback edition through IngramSpark as well, and my eBook through Smashwords and Draft2Digital. I will explain below how this can happen and what I see as the relevant virtues, or constraints, of using each of these providers.

Print Publications

IngramSpark

IngramSpark offers a print-on-demand service for authors that has many similarities to that offered by Amazon KDP. Amazon KDP, however, dominates the market and will almost certainly generate a higher volume of sales for your publication. IngramSpark's publishing processes can also seem a little 'clunky' in comparison to the ease of working through the publishing process with Amazon.

Despite this, in my view, there are two reasons for publishing your book with IngramSpark. The first is that they fill a gap Amazon KDP has not yet filled themselves — they publish hardbacks, as well as the normal offering of paperbacks and eBooks.

The second, and more compelling, reason is that they seem to be the provider of choice for some online booksellers and most 'bricks-and-mortar' booksellers (i.e. those with physical stores), libraries and academic institutions. Amazon's approach to royalties, in particular, has inclined many of these groups to prefer IngramSpark as their source of print-on-demand paperbacks.

The differing approaches to setting royalties by Amazon and IngramSpark means that with IngramSpark, you have the flexibility to set terms that are more attractive to booksellers. It also means that you have the potential to make more per book sale with IngramSpark. Amazon, nonetheless, has far greater reach than IngramSpark and will almost certainly generate a much greater volume of sales. My preference, therefore, is to publish with IngramSpark as an *addition* to working with Amazon, rather than as an alternative.

I won't spend time in this publication walking you through the IngramSpark publishing process as I have done for the Amazon KDP process. Once you have been through Amazon's process, you should be able to find your way through IngramSpark's process, even if it seems 'clunky' in comparison. Simply go to ingramspark.com, click on Create an Account, and follow your nose from there. They also have a useful User Guide, which you should download, that will help you navigate your way.

You need to be aware that, unlike Amazon, IngramSpark, in addition to taking a share of any royalties from sales, does require a US$49 upfront fee per publication. You don't pay this until you commence the process of creating a book, so it costs you nothing simply to open an account in the first place. Paying a fee for every publication, of course, means that if you publish both a paperback and a hardback edition through them, you will pay that fee twice.

It is also worth noting that a hardback publication is considered a separate publication, no matter who publishes it for you (there are other providers, such as Lulu, who do hardbacks, not just IngramSpark). It therefore requires its own ISBN, different to the one you may have used for your paperback.

With regard to the paperback, however, as long as you didn't opt for Amazon KDP's offer of Extended Distribution when you published a paperback with them, you can use that same ISBN for the paperback you publish with IngramSpark.

One other issue with producing a hardback edition is the cover requirements. While the manuscript file can be almost exactly the same as that used for a paperback (just make sure you have updated the ISBN to show the correct one for the hardback, or better still, list both ISBNs on the Copyright page of all of your print manuscript files), the cover file will need some tweaking. The two options for how the cover is produced by IngramSpark — either using a 'dust jacket' that wraps around the board that forms the cover or laminating the cover onto that board — both require a larger cover than that used for a paperback of the same trim size. An experienced cover designer should be able to deal with this requirement fairly easily, and for a very low fee, as should an experienced amateur. If you don't fit into either of those categories, you will have to get someone to help you make the necessary changes to your cover file.

IngramSpark will also publish an eBook for you. Personally, I can see nothing to be gained by doing that if you have already published an eBook with Amazon KDP. See the following for my advice about additional publishers for your eBook.

eBook Publications

Once you have published your eBook with Amazon KDP, and after you have allowed your participation in KDP Select to come to an end, assuming you enrolled in that service for a period of time (the minimum period is three months), you should give serious consideration to publishing your eBook with Smashwords and Draft2Digital as well. Neither of these companies charges an upfront fee (they take what I regard as a reasonable percentage of your royalties on sales instead). They do both require an ISBN for your eBook (something Amazon KDP does not require), but both offer to provide you with an ISBN for free.

Smashwords

Although Draft2Digital is, in my view, a better additional platform to complement distribution of your eBook through Amazon KDP, Smashwords (smashwords.com) has a few very handy features which still make it attractive to authors. Smashwords also has a far greater reach than Amazon, working with a number of online booksellers Amazon doesn't work with, and in many countries Amazon does not reach.

Apple iBooks, to give just one example, which you cannot reach through Amazon if you have opted for KDP Select, sells into over 50 countries, while Amazon sells eBooks into only about a dozen or so (albeit those dozen are the biggest markets). Smashwords distributes through Apple as well as many other online retailers Amazon does not work with. Amazon may have some 70% of the eBook market, but you still want access to the remaining 30% as well.

As Draft2Digital has a similar reach to Smashwords, but are much easier to work with and provide a better author interface, I prefer them over Smashwords. The additional features offered by Smashwords that neither Amazon nor Draft2Digital offer are what still incline me to use Smashwords as well.

As noted above, you pay no upfront fee with Smashwords; they charge a commission on sales, which equates to about 10% of the retail price. They do require an ISBN to publish your eBook but will provide you with one for free. Although they do not require exclusive rights (they place no restriction on you also publishing with any other company), my personal preference means that I still supply my own ISBN. I buy them in a block of 10, which brings the price down to only a handful of dollars each, for this very reason. The choice is yours.

The services they provide which I find useful, particularly when you consider it can cost you nothing to make your eBook available on Smashwords, include:

- Coupons — these can be used by customers to get a free copy of your eBook. They are a very useful marketing and promotional tool which can be offered by you, for example, to contest winners or perhaps to every tenth person that signs on to your mailing list. The possibilities are endless.
- Free Sample — a potential customer can access a free sample of your eBook from your Smashwords Book Page.
- Downloads in various formats — Smashwords offers customers the ability to download your eBook, once they have purchased it, in whatever format they require for their particular eReader. Importantly, you, as the author, can also utilise this function if you want to provide a copy to someone in a format other than that used by Amazon KDP (i.e. MOBI format). Formats available include EPUB, MOBI, PDF, LRF, PDB and TXT.

Draft2Digital

Draft2Digital is similar to Smashwords in that it has no upfront fee, they charge a very reasonable percentage of any royalties, and they do require an ISBN. Like Smashwords, they also offer to provide an ISBN for free. As noted above, they match Smashwords' distribution advantages. Their advantage lies in that they do that more easily than Smashwords does, and with a far better and easier-to-use author and customer interface.

They also provide, through their partnership with Books2Read, an internet page which provides your customers with one gateway to all of the online retailers for your eBook. Have a look at my page for my novel, *As Fire is to Gold*, Book One of the Chronicles of the Ilaroi at https://books2read.com/u/47E88a, to see how this works.

Although I have also published a further publication, which combines Books One and Two of the Chronicles of the Ilaroi into one volume — *As Fire is to Gold: The Complete Chronicles of the Ilaroi* — I have not published the eBook edition of that publication through either Smashwords or Draft2Digital as yet, as I am still utilising my three-month period with KDP Select to take advantage of the attributes that offers.

Overall, in my view, Draft2Digital is a far superior provider to Smashwords. As I like using Smashwords' coupons and find their easy access to downloads of my eBook in whatever format I require so useful, however, I continue to use both of these providers.

7. YOUR SHOPFRONT: AMAZON'S AUTHOR AND BOOK PAGES

Once your book is published through Amazon KDP, Amazon will create a page for your book on its online stores. You will also be able to create an Author Page, but more about that later.

The Amazon Book Page

Linking your Paperback, eBook and other editions

Start with accessing Author Central. This is a place on the Amazon website where authors can manage much of the information about their books as well as create and manage a page about themselves as Author (more on the Author Page below). Amazon will advise you how to access Author Central in one of their initial emails confirming that your book has now been published on their stores.

If you have published both a paperback and an eBook edition, you should, in fact, have two Book Pages already — one for each of these editions. Click on the 'Books' tab on Author Central and add your book (or books). Assuming you have linked both publications on your Bookshelf, Amazon should recognise this, and the pages for the two editions of your book should be linked, with a simple click allowing a customer to switch from one to the other edition, depending on their preferences.

This linking may take a few days to happen. If after three days or so, it has not occurred, contact Amazon through their Help email address and ask them to fix the link for you. You should find a 'Contact Us' link near the bottom of some of the pages in Author Central. They are usually very helpful with matters such as this and usually respond fairly quickly.

Should you later decide to create a hardback edition through IngramSpark, on request, Amazon can create a link to that as well (in my case, they updated this without any need for me to request them to do so). Similarly, should you decide to also create a large-print edition, that can be linked to your other editions too. In short, all of your editions of the same book, as well as any hardback edition created through IngramSpark, should be able to be linked on your Amazon Book Pages. This will not only look more professional than otherwise unconnected pages, but it will also make it easier for customers to select the edition they are looking for.

Updating your Book Page(s)

The Books tab in Author Central also enables you to update some of the information that will appear on your Book Page(s). Have a look at what your page contains and update any information as you feel necessary.

Be aware, however, that if you amend the Book Description through Author Central, and then subsequently amend some other aspect of your publication, such as by uploading a revised and updated version of your manuscript or your cover (as described in Step 12), when those changes are accepted by Amazon, whatever is in your Book Description on your Book Page will be replaced by what is in the Book Description field on your Bookshelf.

The way to avoid this happening is: whenever you update your Book Description through Author Central, also update the Book Description field on your Bookshelf. There is no need to republish through the Bookshelf if that is all you are changing, simply save the update so that if and when you do republish at any later date, the correct and updated version of your Book Description will be applied.

You should also go back and have a look at what I said under Step 6 about how to include formatting into your Book Description. You can use the method outlined there as a substitute for the rudimentary formatting options open to you through Author Central.

Creating a Serial Page

If your book is part of a series, you can ask Amazon to create a Series Page for you. When I published my fantasy tale, the Chronicles of the Ilaroi, I split the work in two due to its length and published it as two separate books. I then asked Amazon to create a series page for me, which they did. It took a few days for it to be done, but I was very happy with the result. You can have a look at my series page at:

https://www.amazon.com/gp/product/B07QJ1L5VM?ref_=dbs_r_series &storeType=eBooks.

The Amazon Author Page

As noted above, Author Central is also the place where you can add information about yourself as an author, which can then be accessed by potential customers. Simply click on the Author Page tab and add whatever information you choose to. Options include:

- your bio
- a link to your author website if you have one
- a photo or photos
- any videos you may have created to promote your book(s)
- a link to your blog, if you have one; this is particularly useful as it will update each time you add a new blog entry on your blog site.

If you wish to, you can also link any publications you have issued under a 'pen name' to your author account. The following article by Publishing With Kindle provides some easy to follow instructions about how to do this: http://publishingwithkindle.com/working-with-amazon-author-pen-names/.

---

8. YOUR OTHER SHOPFRONT: YOUR AUTHOR WEBSITE

Your Amazon Book Page is just one of your shopfronts. Your Author Website is another. You don't have to have an author website, of course. After all, you have an Author Page on Amazon. But what about all the other online retailers which will eventually list your book? They are not going to refer their customers to your Amazon pages. And then there's anyone who comes across your name as an author in some other way — at a book launch, for example, or after seeing a review of your book in the local newspaper perhaps.

An author page provides an excellent platform for showcasing both you and your work, particularly if you are in the writing business for the long haul. It can be a place where potential customers, or fans, or people who have already read your book can go to find out more about you, to read about what you are working on as your next project, or simply to find out where they can purchase your book.

Have a look at my author website as just one example (https://markmccabeauthor.com), or Google some of your favourite authors and have a look at their sites and what sort of information they put on them. The approaches taken by authors are many and varied. The following are just a few of the ideas for things you could include on your site.

- Your bio.

- Your books and link to the places where customers can purchase their various editions - e.g. the paperback edition, the eBook, a hardback edition, a large print edition (if you have the latter two).
- Links to any other works you might have published previously (e.g. a short story, or stories).
- Details of any awards or reviews of your work that you are proud of.
- Some information about any other writing projects you are working on.
- More detail about your books than what is offered in the publications themselves (e.g. a fantasy author may provide additional maps, or some of the back-stories to the world or nations they have used for their novel(s)).
- A blog.
- A sign-up page so that fans can be added to your mailing list (such a list can be invaluable when you publish your next book!).
- Links to any Twitter, Facebook, Instagram, YouTube or any other social media presence you have.
- A Contact page which lets people know how they can email you with questions or comments (apart from anything else, this can be a good source of information about spelling errors and the like which may have escaped your editing net).

Your first thought may be that you can't afford an author website. That's a fair call. Be aware, however, that anyone who is prepared to put the time in can get themselves a very professional-looking website at a relatively low cost these days.

There are many ways to go about acquiring a website. Do a bit of research on the internet and you will quickly find you are spoilt for choice. I use WordPress for my site. Although at first glance, WordPress may appear to be only a blogging platform, that is incorrect. It can be used for straightforward sites just as easily. For a relatively small fee per annum (less than $100), WordPress offers a wide range of templates many of which, with a minimum of effort, can be quickly configured into something that suits your needs. An even wider range of templates becomes available for a further upgrade (and a further fee). WordPress will also provide you with an internet address and will 'host' your site for yet a further fee (once again, somewhere around the $100 to $150 mark, depending on what you opt for) per annum.

For my site, I purchased my domain name from another service provider, which also hosts my site, but signed up with WordPress so that I could use their software to build and manage the site's content. All up, it costs me around $200 per annum. For that outlay, I was able to build my whole site. I made the 3D mock-ups of my book covers, for example, by going to a site that enabled me to do that for no charge —

https://diybookcovers.com/3Dmockups/.

This is just one of a number of sites that offer that function for free on the internet. There are many other free tools available on the internet specifically designed for those building their own website.

You will see that my site has a little bit about me, a lot more about my books and how to get them, with links to Amazon and other online retailers that stock them, a bit about my current project, and a means of contacting me by email should anyone wish to do so. I also run a blog. Anyone who visits my site can sign up for regular updates which will usually be in the form of an email letting them know whenever I post a new blog.

You don't have to do all of that, however. You may just opt for a few pages — one providing a bit of a bio about yourself, one with information about your book (or books) and where to go to buy a copy, and perhaps one with advice on how to contact you if anyone has any questions.

I am not going to go into any detail about how to build your own website here, other than what I have said above. There are whole books and plenty of websites on the internet about how to do that. As a final note, however, I offer two bits of advice.

- Don't bother getting yourself an author website if you are not going to make it look professional. The whole idea of an author website is to showcase you and your work. Why go to all of the trouble to make your book look every bit as professional as one published by one of the big publishing houses, and then promote it on a website that looks cheap and nasty? A cheap-looking website will say to the world that both you and your work are cheap. Stick with Amazon's author page in that case.

- Be wary of getting your nephew or some similar person to do it for you because 'they know a bit about computers'. See the dot-point above.

---

9. MARKETING AND PROMOTION

As I have noted elsewhere, many believe that publishing your book is simply the end of one project and the beginning of an even larger one — marketing and promotion. The skills and desires which drive us to write a book, however, don't necessarily help us master the art of promoting that very same thing.

Many authors simply don't want to have to be involved in this aspect of being a published author. They say that this is the very reason they want to find a traditional publisher. They want someone to look after all that marketing and promotion 'stuff' for them.

Unfortunately, securing a traditional publisher, if you are one of those rare few authors that do so, doesn't necessarily mean that you can ignore marketing and promotion and get back to the business of writing while your publisher looks after such matters. In fact, one of the most common gripes from traditionally published authors is about how little their publisher does for them in terms of marketing.

Whether you are traditionally published, or self-published, if you want to be a successful author, you simply have to engage in this side of the business. How far you do so will be up to you. There is a wide range of activities you can engage in to promote your work. Most authors engage in some of these, some do almost nothing, and a very few engage in all of them, along with other activities I haven't even thought of or mentioned here.

Let me outline just a few of them here in order to broaden your knowledge of some of the avenues available for you to promote your work. Though I will just touch on most of these here, there is a wealth of information available on each and every aspect of marketing and promoting books — from whole books on the subject to innumerable useful articles available on the internet.

Amazon's Book and Author Pages

I have already discussed both of these avenues in Chapter 7. As they will be the portal most of your online customers will go through, you simply must pay attention to these pages. If you do nothing else, set them up properly in the first place.

In an ideal world, you would also refresh these from time to time, perhaps giving them a new look or reviewing the content so that they stay relevant to your likely customers.

Your Author Website

This has already been discussed in Chapter 8. I believe an author website is a must in the modern world, and it is not hard to have a professional-looking website for a relatively low outlay of funds. You don't have to include all of the material some authors do; the basics will do if that is all you can commit to. Better that than committing to a vast array of information that quickly becomes out-of-date as you struggle to keep up with the demands of refreshing it.

Business Cards

Business Cards can be very cheap to have printed (perhaps around $40 or so for 250 cards) and can be very useful to hand out to anyone who expresses an interest in your publication. Put your author website details on them, if you have one, along with an email address or other preferred way of contacting you. If you don't have a website, try to include the title of your publication so that someone can easily find it on Amazon or wherever else it is available for sale.

Consider using some of the artwork from your publication's cover as a background for the cards.

A Book Launch

A book launch can be a great way of creating some initial attention and a bit of a 'buzz' that helps spread the word about your publication. It may even attract the attention of local media (perhaps radio or local press) and snowball into something more useful than just the launch itself.

If you're lucky, one of the more established of your local bookstores may be the ideal venue for an event like this. They may have hosted launches before for other authors. If so, they will know exactly what is required and will have experience in helping to make it happen. Even better if this becomes an opportunity to ask them to stock a few copies of your book and perhaps sell some on the day. This is where author copies (see Chapter 5) can become really useful.

There are plenty of articles on the internet about how to run a book launch and the types of things you will need to make it happen.

Book Reviews

If you think back to what I said under Step 4, you will remember the importance I gave to book reviews. To reiterate, I indicated that the most important influences on a potential customer's decision regarding whether to purchase your book were, in descending order:

- the author's reputation or what they already know about the author
- the book's cover
- the 'blurb' on the back of the cover or the description on the Amazon Book Page
- good reviews from other readers or from authors of note.

Reviews are, unfortunately, a two-edged sword. While many customers will be reluctant to consider purchasing a book that hasn't been reviewed, bad reviews will also repel them. You simply have to take your chances in this regard. Have a look at some of the strategies for trying to get some reviews and see which, if any, of those might suit you.

You will find that there are no guaranteed strategies, either to get reviews at all or to get good ones. While you have the choice regarding which if any reviews to promote, either on the book's cover, its description on Amazon, or through your author website, sites such as Amazon and Goodreads will simply display them all, or at least will display an average of all of the scores that reviewers have allocated to your work. They are also alert to attempts by authors to 'stack' or otherwise influence the ratings, through offers of, say, a free download of the book in exchange for a favourable review, or by authors creating a multiple number of logins to lodge fake reviews.

A Blog

Consider posting regular blogs, perhaps about the genre you are writing in or writing in general, or just about matters of interest to you individually. Include in your sign-off for each blog a link to either your author website, your Amazon author page or some similar internet address that directs followers to your work.

A Mailing List

If you have a website or a blog, consider including a Mailing List sign-up page. Products like MailChimp (www.mailchimp.com) provide a range of tools, including the capacity to add mail list sign-up pages to your website, along with an automated response, at no cost. Advanced functionality does attract a fee but probably won't become necessary unless you start to develop a big following, in which case you will be well on your way to becoming a successful author.

When you are preparing to publish your next book, you will find a Mailing List of potential customers an invaluable aid in either building pre-publication hype or alerting those people once the publication is available for purchase, or both.

Facebook

While I am no huge fan of Facebook's current approach to the use of data they collect, or their policies in respect of some of the types of material that can be distributed on their sites, they simply are an indispensable tool for authors trying to spread the word about their work.

There are many sites that help authors either share information with potential customers or engage with other writers about issues they are confronting. You don't have to open up your life so that everyone knows what you had for breakfast and just what it tasted like. Use it carefully and responsibly and only share as much or as little about yourself as you want to. Make the primary focus be about your writing.

Goodreads

If you don't know much about Goodreads, then I suggest you have a look at their site. People can engage with Goodreads as a reader, or as an author, or both. Sign-on and then claim your publication as the author. It can be a good way of getting those all-important reviews and has a few interesting marketing tools of its own.

Google some of the articles on the internet about how to use Goodreads as a marketing tool as an author.

Twitter

Twitter is another vehicle for disseminating information about your publications as widely as you can. It is not hard to use (just ask Donald Trump) and can be quickly added to your array of promotional tools. If you are already on Twitter, consider creating a specific author 'handle' to separate your promotional tweets from whatever else you may want to tweet about as an individual.

My own view is that it is best to keep your author tweets relatively free of political, religious or other comments, but I do sometimes find it difficult not to slip into retweeting some of the messages I think are particularly important.

One piece of advice here that is also relevant to most of the other social media platforms is not to respond to comments that are critical of you or your work. Twitter 'trolls', once they turn their focus upon you, can make your life a misery, and they will always have the last word. The best strategy is to count to ten (perhaps 100) and then ignore such comments or stick solely to factual responses.

Instagram

Many authors use an Instagram account as yet another way to promote their work. As I haven't ventured into the world of Instagram thus far, I won't offer any advice in this regard. Suffice to say that there are many articles on the internet about how best to use Instagram to promote your work as an author.

YouTube

YouTube also offers opportunities for authors to promote their work. You might, for example, create your own channel and post occasional readings from your book(s), perhaps with a static background of your book's cover, or simply discuss issues or thoughts associated with your genre or with writing as a craft. The possibilities here are probably many and varied.

Podcasts

As with YouTube, this is yet another vehicle to promote your work. There are many articles on the web about how to create and post podcasts.

Amazon Ads

Amazon Ads can be a useful way to market your book. They can also consume funds at a rapid rate if not handled with care. Amazon Ads fall into two basic categories:

- sponsored ads
- lockscreen ads.

Sponsored ads promote products to shoppers actively searching using related keywords or viewing similar products on Amazon. Lockscreen ads are based on shoppers' interests and are shown when they 'unlock' their Kindle E-readers or Fire Tablets to begin reading or shopping for books.

Both options allow you to set your budget and the duration of your ad campaign. You also have the capacity to 'hold' or pause a campaign at any point, effectively ending that campaign if you leave it in that state until its duration expires

Have a look at the information supplied on the Amazon KDP site and do some exploration on the internet before venturing into either of these avenues. One good way of testing an ad campaign while also fine-tuning your keywords is as follows.

Create a Sponsored Ad. Research all of the likely keywords that might apply to your genre and your target audience and put as many into your campaign as you can. When I did this, I had nearly 100 keywords. Then set a low daily budget — perhaps $8 or so a day, and run it for four of five days. Have a look at the reports that are available each day and tinker with the allocation per keyword accordingly.

Sponsored ads work by connecting people to your book who have put keywords into their book search on Amazon that match your keywords. It won't take them to your Book Page but will get your publication onto the list of books that match their selection. The strength of your cover, book description and so on will then come into play influencing whether they click on your book and have a closer look at it.

Although you will be competing with other authors who are using similar keywords, you will soon see the small number of keywords out of all of the ones you have input that are matching customers' inputs more frequently than others.

Even if you generate no actual sales from such a short campaign, you can use the results to replace the keywords you initially used on your Bookshelf with ones that are more likely to draw your book to customers' attention.

Remember one thing if you remember nothing else about Amazon Ads (or any other ads for that matter). They are all about getting your book in front of customers' eyes. They do not guarantee sales in themselves. The merits of your book, its cover, the blurb, reviews, its price, and the like will then determine whether a customer will take the next step and consider purchasing it.

Libraries

Getting your book(s) placed in your local library, or even ones much further afield, can be an invaluable way of spreading the word about yourself as an author, as well as your publications. Someone who borrows your book from the library could easily become an avid devotee who then goes out and buys all of your existing and any future publications.

In some countries, a fund is created, which is then dispersed amongst local authors whose books are borrowed by library members. Although the amount likely to be received from such funds will undoubtedly be small, it should be considered. You can read more about Libraries in Chapter 11.

Local Bookstores

I mentioned local bookstores above under Book Launches. You can also ask local bookstores to put your books on their shelves and sell them for you. If you succeed in gaining their cooperation, they are likely to ask for only two or three copies to start with to see how they go.

The best approach is not to turn up at the bookstore unannounced. Ring first and find out who is responsible for their acquisitions and see if you can make an appointment to go in and discuss the matter with them. Be professional and objective about your publication and go armed to such meetings with certain items. These include:

- a New Title Information sheet or 'Sell Sheet'. Do a search on the internet for the sort of information to include on such a sheet, which is usually confined to one page

- your business card

- three copies of your book so that you can 'strike while the iron is hot' if they agree at the conclusion of the meeting

- an invoice for payment for the three books (noting, when you set a price for the bookstore to pay you, that they will likely need to add 40% to whatever you charge them when setting the price they will sell it at to their customers)

- a précis of what you are doing to promote the book in their area or region (e.g. a book launch, interviews on local radio, review in the local newspaper, a reading at the library, etc.).

10. ROYALTIES AND REPORTS

How royalties are calculated and how you can track sales and what you earn are, of course, critical considerations for authors. Amazon KDP provides a range of resources to assist authors in monitoring their earnings.

Printed Publications (Paperback)

Pricing & Royalty

The third sub-page of your Bookshelf entry, Paperback Rights & Pricing, is where you determine what profit, if any, you will make from your book.

List Price

Usually, an author sets a List Price (that is, the price at which Amazon will sell your book, noting that in some countries, some form of VAT may still be added to that price) for the US market (Amazon.com) and then lets Amazon KDP derives the price for their six other marketplaces from that figure. Before doing that, you will need to decide whether you will opt for:

- the standard distribution deal, which will give you a Royalty of 60%, or
- the expanded distribution deal, which will give you a Royalty of 40%.

To calculate the royalty due, use the following equation:

Royalty = (List Price - Printing Cost) x Royalty Percentage

When you insert a price in the List Price field, Amazon KDP does this calculation for you. This enables you to play around with the List Price until you are happy with the outcome.

Consider comparable costs for books in your genre before settling on a final figure. While a high final royalty may seem attractive, setting a List Price which many customers find unpalatable will inevitably impact on sales.

Once you have settled on a price for the US market, click on '6 other marketplaces' to see how that translates to prices for those countries. You can then vary the prices for any of those markets to make them appear more sensible. You might, for example, change a price for the Australian market from a derived figure of A$21.86 to A$21.99.

eBook Publications

Royalty & Pricing

The Kindle eBook Pricing Page on your bookshelf is where you determine what profit, if any, you will make from sales of your eBook. You can still make adjustments to your pricing after your book is published, but you don't want to confuse or annoy your readers unnecessarily.

70% or 35%

To get a 70% royalty, you must meet a certain number of conditions:

- You must price your eBook between US$2.99 and US$9.99
- You will pay a small fee for file delivery to the customer
- You won't get 70% in all territories, but you will get it in the US and most of Europe
- Your eBook must not be in the public domain

- Your eBook must be part of KDP Select if you want the 70% royalty in Brazil, India, Japan or Mexico
- You must agree to allow buyers to lend their copy of your eBook to friends and family for up to 14 days.

I can't see a good reason not to opt for 70%. I don't enrol in KDP Select after the first three months, however. I am not concerned that this means I won't get 70% in Brazil, India, Japan or Mexico.

List Price

Usually, an author sets a List Price (that is, the price at which Amazon will sell your book, noting that in some countries, some form of VAT or other tax may still be added to that price) for the US market (Amazon.com). They then let Amazon KDP derive the price for their 12 other eBook marketplaces from that figure.

Once you insert a price in the List Price field, Amazon KDP calculates the royalty payable to you depending on which of the two royalty plans you have chosen. This enables you to play around with the List Price until you are happy with the outcome.

A recently added function, Kindle Pricing Support (Beta), let's you see the relationship between the price and past sales and author earnings for KDP books like yours. Selecting this option takes you to a page which displays a graph of the comparisons and suggests a List Price for your book which, based on historic data for KDP books similar to yours, would maximise your author earnings. It remains your choice whether to follow this advice or set a different price.

Regardless of whether you utilise the KDP Pricing Support advice, you should do some research of your own and consider comparable costs for books in your genre before settling on a final figure. While a high final royalty may seem attractive, setting a List Price which many customers find unpalatable will inevitably impact on sales.

Once you have settled on a price for the US market, click on 'Other Marketplaces' to see how that translates to prices for those markets. You can then vary the prices for any of those markets to make them appear more sensible.

Reports

Once your book has been published, you will be able to access reports by clicking on the Reports tab that sits beside the Bookshelf tab when you log in to Amazon KDP. Many of these reports will be available online, and some will also be available for download and print by clicking on a button labelled 'Generate'. The tabs available from the Reports page include:

- Sales Dashboard – providing the most commonly sought data for the past three months, including:
  o Units (publications) Ordered
  o Kindle Edition Normalised pages (KENP) read from KU (Kindle Unlimited) and KOLL (Kindle Owners' Lending Library)
  o Royalties Earned
- Historical – providing historical data on the items under the Sales Dashboard
- Month-to-Date
- Payments
- Pre-orders
- Promotions
- Prior Months' Royalties
- Ad Campaigns.

You should familiarise yourself with the various reports available, utilising the extensive Help text wherever necessary.

11. LIBRARIES

One way to spread the word about you and your publications is by getting your book placed in libraries. In some countries, authors can even be eligible for a small payment for each occasion their book is borrowed from a library, but don't count on getting rich this way; the payment will most likely be very small.

Some national libraries also require local authors to legally 'deposit' a copy of any new publication so that the library can be assured of holding a copy of every book that has been published by one of their citizens (see more on this below).

IngramSpark

In Chapter 6 of this book, I talked about some of the reasons for considering publishing your paperback with IngramSpark once it has been published through Amazon KDP. One of the reasons is IngramSpark seem to be the provider of choice for many libraries. In part at least, this seems to be because Amazon's approach to royalties has enabled IngramSpark to position themselves as a more cost-effective distributor to libraries.

Do some internet searches to identify the primary library suppliers in your country and see if you need to register your publication with them. Talk to your national writers' association or have a look on their website. They will usually know exactly how this works in your country and should be able to tell you what you need to do to make your publication available.

Approaching libraries

You can, of course, approach local libraries directly, with a high chance of them being receptive to the idea of stocking your book. The best way to do this is to phone them first, if for no other reason than to find out exactly who at the library you need to talk to — it will probably be their acquisitions person.

If they aren't prepared to spend a few dollars to buy it, consider offering the library a free copy. Although you may think that you are undercutting potential sales by this approach, you are actually creating an opportunity to spread the word about your work.

Once you do get your book into the local library, consider approaching the library and offering your services for an author talk. These events are popular with library users and provide an opportunity for writers to connect with their readers. Sometimes libraries are able to pay a small fee, but mostly the author donates their time free, and the event is free of cost to attendees.

When you approach a library, the staff will probably need the following information: your name, the title of your book, your CV, website, reviews, details of previous speaking experience, photograph, availability for dates and times. Once the event has been agreed, generally the library itself will promote it to the community. There will often be an opportunity to sell books to people who attend the talk on the day. Those author copies might come in handy after all.

National Libraries and 'Legal Deposit'

In some countries, the law requires authors to provide a copy (in some cases two or even three copies) of any new publication to the national library, so that it can fulfil its goal of holding at least one copy of every work published in that country. Although I would be surprised to hear that anyone has ever been fined for not doing this, apart from complying with the law, this is a good way of ensuring your book's survival for many years (centuries?) to come.

The following links may help you find out what the requirements are in your country.

- **Australia** - National Library of Australia (https://www.nsla.org.au/resources/topic/legal-deposit)
- **Canada** - Library and Archives Canada (https://www.bac-lac.gc.ca/eng/services/legal-deposit/Pages/legal-deposit.aspx)
- **New Zealand** - National Library of New Zealand (https://natlib.govt.nz/publishers-and-authors/legal-deposit)
- **United Kingdom** - British Library (https://www.bl.uk/help/how-to-deposit-your-digital-publications)
- **USA** - United States Copyright Office at the Library of Congress

Wikipedia offers a fuller list of countries with their Legal Deposit requirements —

https://en.wikipedia.org/wiki/Legal_deposit#United_States.

Copyright Registration

When searching for information about legal deposit for libraries, be aware of predatory 'copyright registration' businesses. These usually exist only to fleece content creators. Usually, registration of copyright is not necessary. It is declared on your Copyright page. Check the way the big publishers in your country do it or check with your national writers' association if you are in any doubt.

---

12. WHY YOU NEED TO WRITE ANOTHER BOOK

Think back to Chapter 1 and what your goals were when you decided to write a book and get it published. If your goal was just that — to finish a book and get it published — then by following the advice in this book, you will have achieved it.

You might, however, have had broader goals. Perhaps you hoped to use this first book as the platform for a career as a writer, or at the very least as the first of several books or publications, the ideas for which may even now be swirling around in your thoughts.

In that case, you need to get on with it and start on your next writing project. Don't wait for your first book to become a success before you invest any more time and effort as a writer. Only a rare few make much of an impression with their first publication, and some of those never go on to write anything else despite that first success.

Successful writing careers tend to be built off the back of a portfolio of work. Can you imagine an artist trying to build a career from just one painting? Of course not. Writing is no different. I noted earlier in this book that writing is a craft. And just like any other craft, most writers develop and hone their skills as they produce more and more output.

Traditional publishers know this. That is why they will generally take proposals from authors with a portfolio of work behind them far more seriously than those who are trying to hawk their first novel. That is just one of the reasons so many authors are turning to self-publishing as a means of kick-starting their careers.

Readers know it too. Many potential customers are wary of authors with just one book to their name. Not all customers see it this way, of course, but many do. A portfolio of work not only suggests you know what you are doing, but it also indicates that if the reader likes one of your books, there will then be the opportunity for them to read another of your publications, if not several.

This creates an interesting dilemma in my favoured genre — fantasy. Many readers of fantasy novels love series. Once they immerse themselves in a fantasy world, some want to be able to wallow around it, to soak up more and more of its ambience. One book is often not enough for them to satiate that need.

The dilemma lies in the fact that, despite the tendency to favour series as opposed to stand-alone stories, many of these same readers refuse to buy the first, or even the second, book in a series when the remaining books have not yet been published. They don't want to have to wait months at the very least, if not years, before the conclusion to the story that has drawn them in becomes available.

What does an author who is writing a series do? Do they publish each book as they finish it, with the promise of more to come? Or do they wait what may take several years to finish the lot and then publish them all at once, or in very rapid succession? While the latter option has its attractions, in the meantime, unless they can keep tantalising their readers by releasing teasers on their website (as George R.R. Martin seems to do so well), they run the risk of their fans drifting away in the meantime.

Regardless of whether you are writing stories that unfold over a series, or stand-alone novels or books, promote your most recent publication, by all means. Develop some marketing knowledge and skills and invest some time and effort in building sales. But at the same time, get on with the business of writing.

Your next project doesn't have to be a novel, of course, assuming that is what you have written. Short stories can be an excellent addition to your oeuvre as well. While the art of writing them is very different from the requirements for writing a novel, learning to write a good short story is a great way of honing your skills.

You might even branch out and try something different altogether — perhaps a different genre, or a different form. While my initial publications were fantasy stories, and I am currently working on a new fantasy series, the idea for this non-fiction publication came out of left-field.

Knowing what they did of my experience to date, my local writing group asked me to do a presentation on self-publishing. I drew up some notes on what I had learnt about the process and subsequently delivered a short presentation on the subject at one of the group's meetings. My notes were then filed away.

A few months later, the thought occurred to me that with my notes, I had the beginnings of a non-fiction book that could be useful to other indie authors. I created a Scrivener file (something I do whenever an idea for a book or story comes along) and moved my notes into there. Having done that, once again, I put the idea aside for later consideration.

In the meantime, I had a look at the range of publications available on the subject and came to the conclusion that many of them were too general. While high-level knowledge was important, I felt that there would be a great benefit in combining that with the more pragmatic instructions needed to navigate one's way through the self-publishing process. And so, I set my fantasy series aside for a brief while and set about compiling this book.

Your own source of inspiration for what to work on next will be as varied as are the sources for all of those other authors out there currently working on their next project or projects. Whatever it is, you know now that you have it within you to take a writing project all the way from initial inspiration right through to a published work.

Get cracking! Life is short.

OTHER PUBLICATIONS

www.ingramcontent.com/pod-product-compliance
Lightning Source LLC
Chambersburg PA
CBHW072133020426
42334CB00018B/1788